CAMBRIDGE LIBRARY COLLECTION

Books of enduring scholarly value

Travel and Exploration

The history of travel writing dates back to the Bible, Caesar, the Vikings and the Crusaders, and its many themes include war, trade, science and recreation. Explorers from Columbus to Cook charted lands not previously visited by Western travellers, and were followed by merchants, missionaries, and colonists, who wrote accounts of their experiences. The development of steam power in the nineteenth century provided opportunities for increasing numbers of 'ordinary' people to travel further, more economically, and more safely, and resulted in great enthusiasm for travel writing among the reading public. Works included in this series range from first-hand descriptions of previously unrecorded places, to literary accounts of the strange habits of foreigners, to examples of the burgeoning numbers of guidebooks produced to satisfy the needs of a new kind of traveller - the tourist.

Across Yunnan

Published posthumously in 1910, Archibald Little's memoir of his journey across the Yunnan Province in Southwest China was one of the first comprehensive accounts of the region to be published in English. Little, a skilled linguist, worked as a merchant in China for over fifty years and opened up the Upper Yangtze area to steam-powered commerce. He was well known for his intrepid travels into territories not yet explored by Westerners, and his record of this journey was originally published as a series of letters to the *North China Herald*. This book also contains Little's account of the building of the French Railway Line to Yunnan-Fu, which provided a trade route from India to the Upper Yangtze region. *Across Yunnan* was completed and edited by Little's wife after his death in 1908. The book includes a detailed map of the area and several photographs.

Cambridge University Press has long been a pioneer in the reissuing of out-of-print titles from its own backlist, producing digital reprints of books that are still sought after by scholars and students but could not be reprinted economically using traditional technology. The Cambridge Library Collection extends this activity to a wider range of books which are still of importance to researchers and professionals, either for the source material they contain, or as landmarks in the history of their academic discipline.

Drawing from the world-renowned collections in the Cambridge University Library, and guided by the advice of experts in each subject area, Cambridge University Press is using state-of-the-art scanning machines in its own Printing House to capture the content of each book selected for inclusion. The files are processed to give a consistently clear, crisp image, and the books finished to the high quality standard for which the Press is recognised around the world. The latest print-on-demand technology ensures that the books will remain available indefinitely, and that orders for single or multiple copies can quickly be supplied.

The Cambridge Library Collection will bring back to life books of enduring scholarly value (including out-of-copyright works originally issued by other publishers) across a wide range of disciplines in the humanities and social sciences and in science and technology.

Across Yunnan

A Journey of Surprises

ARCHIBALD JOHN LITTLE
EDITED BY ALICIA LITTLE

CAMBRIDGE
UNIVERSITY PRESS

CAMBRIDGE UNIVERSITY PRESS

Cambridge, New York, Melbourne, Madrid, Cape Town, Singapore,
São Paolo, Delhi, Dubai, Tokyo, Mexico City

Published in the United States of America by Cambridge University Press, New York

www.cambridge.org
Information on this title: www.cambridge.org/9781108014090

This edition first published 1910
This digitally printed version 2010

ISBN 978-1-108-01409-0 Paperback

This book reproduces the text of the original edition. The content and language reflect
the beliefs, practices and terminology of their time, and have not been updated.

Cambridge University Press wishes to make clear that the book, unless originally published
by Cambridge, is not being republished by, in association or collaboration with, or
with the endorsement or approval of, the original publisher or its successors in title.

The original edition of this book contains a number of colour plates, which cannot
be printed cost-effectively in the current state of technology. The colour scans
will, however, be incorporated in the online version of this reissue, and in printed
copies when this becomes feasible while maintaining affordable prices.

Additional resources for this publication at www.cambridge.org/9781108014090

ACROSS YUNNAN

By Mr. Davidson.

Irrigating Wheel.

Frontispiece.

ACROSS YUNNAN:

A Journey of Surprises

Including an Account of the
Remarkable French Railway Line
now completed to Yunnan-fu

BY
ARCHIBALD LITTLE

AUTHOR OF

"THROUGH THE YANGTSE GORGES"
"TO MOUNT OMI AND BEYOND"
"THE FAR EAST"

EDITED BY
MRS. ARCHIBALD LITTLE

WITH MANY ILLUSTRATIONS AND MAP

LONDON
SAMPSON LOW, MARSTON & CO., LTD.
1910

EDITORIAL NOTE

ORIGINALLY written as letters to the *North China Herald*, of which my husband's brother, R. W. Little, was then the Editor, and now for the first time published in England by the kind permission of the present Editor, this volume lacks the final corrections of the author; although in Shanghai he wrote the intro-duction here given. Before publishing it in book form he wished, I think, to add to it and somewhat to remodel it. But the time for that never came.

Now, however, that the French have so far com-pleted their railway from Hanoi to Yunnan-fu, that it is to be officially opened on April 1st, 1910, I have done my very imperfect best to revise the volume, as I think my husband would have wished, and to bring it out also in April as a tribute to that French enterprise on which he touches so often with warm admiration in these pages. Had he lived, I know what valuable additions they would have gained from his richly-stored memory and original tone of thought; whereas I could but diminish the value of what he has written by additions. Regarded as his freshly-written impressions of our last travel together in China, the following pages will, I hope, convey to the reader something of his intense enjoyment at the time.

I must acknowledge the kindness of Major H. R. Davies in allowing use to be made of a portion of the valuable map at the end of his "Yunnan, the link between India and the Yang-tse" (Cambridge University Press), in place of the rough outline map sketched at the time by the Author, as also of Major D. Fraser's help in the matter.

ITINERARY

LAND ROUTE FROM SUI-FU TO YUNNAN-FU

	MILES.	STAGES.
Sui-fu to Szechuan Border	60	4
Szechuan Border to Lao-wa-t'an..	20	2
Lao-wa-t'an to Chao-tung	132	6
Chao-tung to Tung-chuan	107	5
Tung-chuan to Yunnan-seng ..	152	7
	471	24

YUNNAN-FU TO HONGKONG

	MILES.	STAGES.
Land journey from Yunnan-fu to Mêng-tse, via the Y-liang defile and the Chen-kiang lake, 720 li, say	215	12
Land journey from Mêng-tse to Man-hao, 130 li, say	39	2
Man-hao to Lao-kai, by Red River..	70	1
N.B.—The distance by the new direct alignment from Yunnan-fu to Lao-kai is 448·2 kilometers = miles 280.	319	15
Lao-kai to Yen-bay by Red River ..	91	1
Yen-bay to Hanoi do.	115	1
Hanoi to Haiphong by rail	62	1
N.B.—The distance by the railway direct from Lao-kai to Haiphong will be 395 kilometers = miles 247.	268	3
Haiphong to Hongkong, via Pak-hoi, Hoi-how, and Kwang-chow-wan, by sea	580	4
	1,167	22

INTRODUCTION

Yunnan is situated in the S.W. corner of the Chinese Empire proper and is a mountain-covered plateau,—not a simple tableland or " Hochebene," as is the Mongolian plateau in greater part. It averages 5,000 feet above the sea-level in the actual and dried-up lake basins that yield a limited level area between the mountains, and 8 to 10,000 feet in its innumerable mountain crests ; whereby is indicated the general ancient level of the whole plateau. It may be classed as a S.E. peninsular extension of the high Tibetan plateau to which it is directly attached on its N.W. border. It is the third largest province of the empire and covers an area of 108,000 square miles. Compare Great Britain with 88,000 square miles and Tonking with 50,000. In situation and climate it bears a marked analogy to that of the high plateau of Mexico, the mean temperature of which likewise ranges from 60° to 70° (the extremes being 50° to 86°). The new French Railway from Haiphong to Yunnan-fu may be compared with that from Vera Cruz to Mexico, which rises 8,000 feet in 263 miles with gradients of 2.51 per 100. The population was estimated by Davenport in 1877 to have fallen, in consequence of the ruthless extermination of the Mahomedans and the mutual massacres of the contending parties, from the original estimate in 1850 of 6,000,000, to about 1,000,000. But, owing to the great recuperative powers of the Chinese, as well as by immigration from over-populated Szechuan and from the adjoining province of Kweichow, the population is now believed to have increased, during the generation that has succeeded the suppression of the Mahomedan revolt by the capture of Ta-li-fu in January, 1873, to about 12,000,000,—almost the full number that this rugged province is capable of supporting.

The Yunnan plateau falls abruptly to the valley of the Yangtse to the north, to the valleys of the Mekong, Salween, and Irrawaddy on the west and to that of the Red River on the south ; involving, in each case, a sudden change from a temperate to a tropical climate, which the inhabitants of the plateau (and *vice versa* those of the border lands) are unable to withstand : hence the isolation of its people. On the east an easier gradient slopes to the basin of the West River of Canton ; this gradient provides the most convenient access to the province and a lively traffic by this route formerly existed, until it was practically closed by the long con-tinued disturbances in the province of Kwangsi and the resultant prevailing brigandage. This traffic has now been diverted to the more roundabout route via the Red River and Tonking. When the intervening country shall have again been restored to orderly government, a railway along the West River valley will provide the easiest and most natural means of access from Canton and Hongkong to the Yunnan plateau.

The general trend of the mountain ranges is from north

to south ; hence the difficulty of entering Yunnan from the Burma side by way of the present trade route from Bhamo to Tali and so on to Yunnan-fu. The intervening rivers run in deep troughs, difficult to cross, while the Tien-shang range west of Tali reaches an elevation of 14,000 feet. The ranges in this north-west corner of the province are, in fact, long spurs running down from the eastern extremity of the great Himalayan range, and alone effectually bar off the province from direct access to the upper valley of the Irrawaddy, and so from Upper Burma. On the other hand, it would appear from recent surveys that, by the line from Mandalay crossing the Salween at the Kun-long ferry, a fairly practicable route, following the north and south trend of the ranges, has been traced up to Ta-li-fu ; and that this western route presents fewer natural difficulties than those which the French are successfully surmounting in the East. But, like the French line, it passes through a very sparsely inhabited country and is thus not likely, for years to come, to pay as a commercial venture ; hence, without some sort of extraneous Government support, there is little prospect of its being built. Yet the supply of Yunnan with the cottons and hardware it now imports in exchange for its opium and mining products, would seem to be worth competing for, even at the cost of some present sacrifice. British manufacturers generally and the merchants of Rangoon in particular, cannot but be interested in the early development of a practicable trade route between Yunnan and Burma ; the only present means of inter-communication being a precarious mule track, dangerous at all times, and impassable in the rainy season, which

connects Tali with Bhamo by the mountain-barred
route via Têng-yueh.

Yunnan lies between the parallels of 21 and 29 latitude
north and between the meridians of 98 and 106 of longi-
tude east : across the province, from Indo-China to the
Yangtse, the plateau extends for a distance of 600 miles.
From Bhamo to Tali the distance is 280 miles, and from
Tali to Yunnan-fu 227 miles. Although, as above
stated, the mountain ranges of Yunnan,—northern
and western Yunnan especially,—run generally north
and south ; yet, through the centre of the province,
uniting the eastern and western capitals,—Yunnan-fu
and Tali,—there runs an ill-defined backbone from which
radiate north and south valleys, on the slopes of which
the streams watering these valleys take their rise.
Hence these 200 miles, separating the two chief cities
of the province, can be bridged by a line following this
backbone with comparative ease ; and presuming, as
is only natural, that Yunnan, the eastern capital, falls
within the French "sphere of influence," while Tali,
the western capital, drops into the British sphere,
then a race will ensue to build this connecting link.
From Yunnan-fu to Man-hao the distance is 255 miles,
thus making the total travel across the province, east
and west from Bhamo to Man-hao, by the existing trade
route, 761 miles. The general formation of the country,
north of Yunnan-fu, as we have told in the account of
our travel, may well be described as "clusters of grey
limestone islands emerging from a sea of red clay "—
the product of their detritus.

Yunnan is bounded on the north by Tibet and Western
Szechuan, on the east by the provinces of Kweichow

and Kwangsi, on the west by the Shan States and Burma,
and on the south by Tonking, the French Laos States,
and the British Shan States of Xientong and Xienhung;
the point of junction where " three Empires meet,"
being on the Mekong river, 30 miles south of the Yunnanese town of Kien-hong.

LIST OF ILLUSTRATIONS

IRRIGATING WHEEL . . . . *Frontispiece*

FACE PAGE

FIRST BREACH IN BARRAGE ACROSS MIN RIVER . 14

WATCH TOWER ON PROVINCIAL BOUNDARY . . 22

CORK-SCREW STAIRCASE UP THE LI-SHAN-TING . 28

STEEP STEPS IN MAIN ROAD 28

KIANG-TI BRIDGE 38

OUTSIDE A YUNNAN TOWN 48

SOLITARY HORSEMAN 48

STONE COLUMN NEAR CHAO-TUNG-FU . . . 60

BULLOCK CART OUTSIDE MÊNG-TSE . . . 60

VICEROY TSEN CHUN-HSUAN WITH HIS TWO LITTLE
SONS 80

SWALLOWS' CAVE FROM TERRACE 110

PACK ANIMALS 110

SWALLOWS' CAVE FROM BELOW 114

GATEWAY ON MÊNG-TSE PASS 122

OPIUM SMOKING 136

ACROSS YUNNAN

PART I

BETWEEN TWO CAPITALS

From May 2—June 12

HAVING found the province of Yunnan and the journey thither very different from my expectations, notwithstanding that I had read almost everything written on the subject, I think others may like to hear more about this unique region and to read the fresh impressions made upon an old traveller in visiting this sequestered corner of the empire. The province of Yunnan is farther of special interest at the moment, since its boundaries have become coterminous with those of the British Indian and of the French Indo-Chinese empires ; and that a race has set in between the two Powers for the development of their respective interests in this land of great potentialities—a race in

which undoubtedly so far our French friends
are a good first.

From the capital of Szechuan to the capital of
Yunnan, a distance of 700 miles by the nearest
road, but of little more than five degrees of
latitude, the time occupied by us in the journey
was exactly forty days. The water in the
branch of the Min river that washes the walls of
the provincial capital being, at the time of our
departure, the end of April, very low, in consequence of the irrigation requirements of the
great Chêngtu plain ; we started out from the
city by the land route to Kia-ting, proceeding
thence by boat to Sui-fu and thence again for
the remainder of the journey by land, there
being in Yunnan no alternative choice of
water carriage such as we find in so many of, if
not all, the other provinces of China, and notably
in the well-watered province of Szechuan.

We travelled to Kia-ting by way of Mei-chou,
a district artificially irrigated in the simple but
marvellously effective manner devised by the
hydraulic engineers of old—the westernmost
arm of the Min river, as it descends from the
high mountains to the north of Kwan-hien, being

By Mrs. Archibald Little.

First Breach in Barrage across Min River at Kwan-hien. This Barrage is removed each year in April and replaced in November.

To face p. 14.

utilised for this region. A barrage of boulder
crates, over one mile in length, laid diagonally
across the stream, holds the water up ten feet
above its natural level and diverts it into a net-
work of channels skilfully planned to cover the
whole plain between Hsin-tsing (New ford) and
Kia-ting, a distance north and south of about
sixty miles.

The vegetation was wonderfully varied in this
district. We saw at once rape being reaped,
buckwheat in full flower and looking like heather
in the distance under clumps of trees, wheat
ripening to harvest, oats and rye ripe, poppy
plants, some in flower, some with their heads
already slashed to extract the opium juice;
groves of trees, fine Nan-mu in fresh green dress,
bamboos sending forth new shoots, funereal
cypress with graceful pendulous branches, alders,
Hoang-ko trees (Ficus Infectoria), and mulberry
trees grown for feeding silk worms. This was
before we took to our boats. The Min river was
very pretty at times, being beautifully wooded,
with many oaks among the trees. We looked
longingly on the road leading to magnificent
Mount Omi, about thirty miles to the west.

Han-yang-fu we found mostly burnt down, through the over-turning of a candle at the worship of the silkworms, thirteen days before. We had twice before passed this way, and, curiously enough, each time found this city mostly burnt down.

From Kia-ting onwards, our progress was agreeably accelerated by a sudden freshet; the Tung river, which descends from Ta-chien-lu and from Ya-chou in two branches, being at the time in spate : we thus made the 100 miles from Kia-ting to Sui-fu at an average speed of seven miles an hour, shooting a constant succession of fierce rapids, and so reaching Sui-fu in one day's journey.

Sui-fu is an important distributing mart, situated at the point of junction of the Min with the Kin-sha,—the "small river" as it is styled by the Sui-fu folk, navigation on the Kin-sha, the main branch of the Yangtse, as marked in our maps, ceasing a short distance above Sui-fu; whereas the Min river, in its different branches, is navigable for hundreds of miles, and is the main channel of communication with Chêngtu and all the wide country to the north and west.

The Min too at this season brings down the larger body of water, until later, in June, the Kin-sha begins to swell, as the monsoon rains gain force in Yunnan and bring about the great summer freshets of the main Yangtse stream. Hence travellers, as well as goods proceeding from Szechuan to Yunnan, take the land road at Sui-fu, which, by way of the Yunnan prefectural cities of Chao-tung and Tung-chuan, leads to Yunnan-fu, in a journey of twenty-four stages,—not including necessary halts to rest the coolies.

With our servants we started from Sui-fu on May 13, a party of twelve carrying coolies, six carrying the great *kangs* of the province, large receptacles into which every kind of thing can be crammed at the last moment; two sedan chairs with eight coolies to carry them, two ponies and our servants' donkey; making our way through crops of large leaved tobacco and poppies, now grown tall and black, and being torn up by the roots. By the side of the road by the river were fine Hoang-ko and ash trees, and on the other bank of the Yangtse we passed by a rock wall recalling the palisades on the Hud-

B

son. The road then follows much the same
direction as does the course of the Kin-sha,—here
pointing nearly due south, and, were this river
navigable, one could proceed by it almost to the
gates of Yunnan-fu, *i.e.*, within two days' long
journey of the capital in latitude 25 north.
As it is, we proceeded by the valley of one of
its affluents, the " Ta-kuan " or " Lao-wa-t'an,"
which runs parallel to that of the Kin-sha,
separated from it by ranges of lofty, sparsely
inhabited mountains; and so we saw nothing
more of the Great River after once having been
ferried across it at the village of Anpien, thirty
miles above Sui-fu. This port of trans-shipment
faces the mouth of the Ta-kuan river, twenty miles
above which the navigation of the Kin-sha entirely
ceases at the city of Ping-shan—Blakiston's
farthest, and the highest limit which the Wood-
cock, one of H.M. light-draft, twin-screw gunboats
ordinarily stationed at Chungking, had succeeded
in reaching.

The road follows up the left bank of the Kin-sha,
through undulating, richly-cultivated country,—
the foothills of the high mountains behind,—
until Anpien is reached. Above this point the

Kin-sha flows in a deep gorge and at Pingshan the
rich foothills merge into the wild mountains,—
inhabited by the independent and inaccessible
Lolo.*

At Anpien we crossed to the right shore of
the Kin-sha, at the point where the river coming
down from Lao-wa-t'an in Yunnan, and commonly
called the Ta-kuan-ho, enters the Yangtse. At the
time of our journey, in May, the Kin-sha was
rolling down thick yellow-ochre coloured water
to join the clearer waters of the Min and its
affluents at Sui-fu ; but·the contribution of the
Ta-kuan, alias Lao-wa-t'an, was transparently
clear, coming from a purely limestone region,
and its contribution added about one-third to the
volume of the Kin-sha. It flows down from the
mountains to the south with a rapid torrent
which would render it unnavigable in any other
country but China. Yet, notwithstanding, we
saw numerous junks of from five to ten tons'
burden and crowded with passengers on their

* Anpien is a dirty little town situated at the confluence of the
Golden or Yangtse River and the Kwan; but we took a pleasant
walk there, and silently and longingly gazed on the further unknown
reaches of the red Yangtse, with the distant mountains beyond, yet
without knowing that we were then taking a final farewell of that
upper Yangtse that had been our home for so many years.
A. E. N. L.

decks descending safely, aided by huge bow-
sweeps. Later on we passed by numerous
wrecks, but goods and passengers encounter
the undoubtedly serious risk in preference to
plodding over the execrable land-trail it was
now our fortune to enter upon.

From Anpien we proceeded up the narrow
valley of the Lao-wa-t'an river, which threads
a devious course between steep, high mountains,
its bed nowhere wider than the actual valley
which the torrent has cut out, and which flows
from the south in a course almost parallel to
that of the Kin-sha further west ;—the latter
here separating the Chinese territory of Szechuan
and Yunnan from that of the independent Lolo
tribes who inhabit the " Terrace of the Sun," the
lofty, almost inaccessible range which here
forms the left bank of the Kin-sha river.   The
right bank of the Kin-sha in this stretch is formed
by a second range of high mountains, running
likewise north and south, which separate its
valley from that of the Ta-kuan, or Lao-wa-t'an
river ; the mountains on both sides running up
in height to ten and twelve thousand feet.   For
ten days we marched steadily up the valley until

the water-parting which forms the natural boundary between the low moisture-laden basin of Szechuan and the high, dry plateau of Yunnan was reached at the head of the Lao-wa-t'an river; but we crossed the political frontier between the two provinces on the third day out from Sui-fu, at the small village of Hsin-chang (Newmarket), where a picturesque side-valley from the east forms the boundary. This is crossed by a handsome many-arched slab bridge and Yunnan is entered. It is not, however, until the city of Ta-kuan, from which the river takes its name, is reached on the ninth day, that the "Red Basin" is left behind and the characteristic vegetation, the banyan and the bamboo, and the warm climate of Szechuan, come to an end. We had now ascended 4,000 feet, and in the evening, in the inn overlooking the torrent, the thermometer, on the 22nd May, showed 86 degrees, whereas after we had entered upon the real Yunnan plateau, it never rose to 80; 70 to 75 degrees being the usual day maximum, even in July, at the commencement of the "Fu-t'ien" or dog-days.

Before we arrived at Lao-wa-t'an we passed by

a cliff on the far or left bank of the river, and in a cleft of the rock in a place now inaccessible, saw a coffin. Afterwards we saw a river gushing forth out of a lofty yellow cavern with stalactites hanging from it, caves in the rock above, and a mountain overhead. At one place we distinguished square holes in the face of the rock, like Meng-liang's ladder on the Yangtse, by which an army is said to have climbed during the night, and so succeeded in overwhelming the other army encamped at the top. After this we came across a number of coffins in inaccessible caves ; in one cave thirteen together. No explanation has yet been discovered of these coffins, nor how or why they were hauled up the face of these lofty cliffs, yet always in sight of the main track. The race that deposited them there seems to have passed away, and with it all records of its existence. The people call them " fairy " coffins.

The city of Ta-kuan-chêng is the capital of the T'ing or district of Ta-kuan (Great Barrier), and once formed the frontier fortress against the wild aborigines,—the Miao-tse and Man-tse, who 1000 and more years ago formed the sole population of Yunnan. The walled city of Ta-kuan is built

By Mrs. Archibald Little.

Watch Tower on the right bank of the Ta-kuan or Lao-wa-t'an River
at Hsin-chang.

To face p. 22.

on the high flat to which the steep ascent from
the valley leads up, and in the midst of an imposing amphitheatre of lofty-fluted limestone
mountains.

Owing to the devious course of the river
and the precipitous gorges in which it is in
parts enclosed, the path fails strictly to follow
its banks, and so has to cross intervening mountain ridges, ascending, and again descending,
3,000 to 4,000 feet, by the most miserable path
masquerading as a high road that it has ever
been my unhappy fate to traverse. Again, when
marching along the valley bottom, it often
happens that a cliff 500 or 600 feet high has
to be surmounted, and in such places a climb,
at first sight seemingly impassable to man or
beast, has to be made over it. Instead of a
short gallery along the face of the cliff itself,
which it would have taken hardly more labour
to cut out, steep steps have been cut up and
down in the hard limestone, so as to surmount
the cliff, and some of these I measured with my
pocket foot-rule and found to be exactly one foot
high and one foot deep,—thus making the path,
in places, an ascent,—and what is still worse,

a descent, at an angle of 45 degrees. And over
this passes the main traffic between the two
rich provinces of Szechuan and Yunnan. The
men of old did good work when they cut out these
steps, but the path has not been relaid for
hundreds of years, and the pack animals have
worn pot-holes, leaving what Coleridge, writing
of German paths a hundred years ago, well calls
"Fangs," and these the sandalled feet of the
coolies (shod with iron clamps beneath) have
polished to a surface of blue glass :—

> "In Koeln, a town of monks and bones,
> And pavements fanged with murderous stones,
> And horrid sights and ghastly wenches,
> I counted two and seventy separate stenches," etc.

We will omit reference to the stenches in
the Chinese inns, which the traveller in China
pays the penalty of enduring night after night,
and draw attention only to the miserable conditions under which trade and traffic have to be
carried on in China to-day. Germany has been
metamorphosed in the past hundred years, but
it needed the shock of a Napoleon to break up
the old régime. Will a like convulsion be needed
in China to rid this magnificent country of the
opium-smoking debauchees who now rule it,

who keep the people in poverty and ignorance, and to whom the word public-spirit is a dead letter ? These thoughts naturally occurred to us as we sat in our sedan-chairs, each of which now had its staff of six coolies, and were carried painfully over paths, upon which we could ourselves neither walk nor ride. Owing to the heavy toil demanded of the coolies, the " chan " or stage is here only eighteen miles in lieu of the usual twenty-seven. The dry winter season is naturally the best for travel, but we were there in the rainy season : notwithstanding that the roads are thus rendered all but impassable, a large traffic was going forward. We met train upon train of coolies carrying the larvæ of the wax insect, raised in Yunnan, for development in Szechuan, where the insect eggs are planted out on forests of Fraxinus sinensis, a species of ash, cultivated for the purpose in the districts of Sui-fu and Kia-ting. Great care has to be taken to prevent premature development en route : the larvæ are carried in paper bags spread upon well-ventilated bamboo trays, and, upon arriving at their destination each night, the carriers have to open out each bag and so

expose the contents to the air. Before turning in
after their hard day's tramp, the coolies have
to repack the parcels, and so have their loads all
ready for an early start the next morning.

We also met long trains of miserable sore-backed
ponies laden with copper, tin, and spelter from
the mines in Yunnan on the way to shipment
down the Yangtse from the port of Sui-fu; the
return loads into Yunnan being largely Sha-si
(Hupeh) cotton cloth and silk hat covers and
"notions" from Szechuan. Needless to say
that the route is strewn with likin stations, which
cause long delays to the porters, there being
large variations in the value of copper cash
and silver between every prefecture we passed
through. Chao-tung boasts 1,400 cash to the
tael (worth now about three shillings), Tung-
chuan-fu 2,000 odd, and Yunnan-fu only 900 odd,
—the cash varying in value according to the
amount of copper they contain, which varies from
nil up to the full quantum; but the great trouble
is that one district will not accept the cash
current in the next, and the traveller has
to make provision or be mercilessly squeezed
accordingly.

The corkscrew ascents by which we mounted
on to the Tibetan plateau presented many striking view points, as, rising into fresh air and
sunshine from the enclosed valley, we paused
and looked down on the rushing river 800 feet
below us. Mimosa trees were opening their
yellow flowers round us, wistaria in blossom;
pomegranate trees, prickly pear, Paotung trees,
bamboos, lovely tallow trees, and the varnish tree
with its dark, rich foliage clothing the rocks.

Although patches of the Szechuan red sandstone are found on the hill-sides, growing rarer
and rarer as one proceeds south, and vanishing
entirely ere the valley of the Ta-kuan river is left
behind, one may classify the whole region from
Sui-fu to Yunnan-fu as a country of rugged
limestone mountains, with valleys between filled
by its weathered detritus. We had been following up a valley, walled in by white cliffs, which
opened out, yielding ground for a city, for the
first time at Lao-wa-t'an : this and the two
prefectural cities of Chao-tung and Tung-chuan
are the only places above the rank of villages
traversed between Sui-fu and Yunnan-fu. At
Lao-wa-t'an ("Cormorant Bar") the river valley

is intersected at right angles by a wider valley
running east and west, and the town is picturesquely situated at the junction. It is a busy place
of about 20,000 inhabitants and possesses a
station of the Bible Christian Mission under
a native pastor, in whose clean dwelling it was
a true pleasure to be received. The town,
which is the head of junk navigation, stands
nearly 2,000 feet above sea level, and 800 feet
above Sui-fu on the Yangtse. Above Lao-wa-t'an
the river is nothing but a roaring torrent, but
with a considerable body of water ; the road
continuing south here crosses it by a handsome
suspension bridge seventy-five yards in length.
At this place porters and teams generally put
in a day's rest, partly to fulfil the demands of
this, the great likin station on the Szechuan-
Yunnan trade route (" La douane la plus productive de la province "—Rocher's *Yunnan*.
Paris, 1880), and well-named " Cormorant
Bar "; partly to prepare for the nine mile, high
pass which is surmounted immediately on leaving
Lao-wa-t'an (the Li Shan Ting,—4,000 feet),
a zigzag ascent cut out in rough steps, descending
from which we find ourselves once more in the

By Mrs. Archibald Little.

Cork-screw Staircase up the Li Shan Ting
(4000 feet).

By Mrs. Archibald Little.

Steep Steps up and down in main road.

To face p. 28.

valley of the Ta-kuan river. The view from the summit roams over a sea of rugged mountains, with smooth-sloping backs and jagged edges, as the strata dip at an angle of 35 from s.s.e. to n.n.w. Patches of purple shale cover in places the general surface of pale brown and brick-red fields of limestone detritus : maize, potatoes (now in flower), together with small fields of stunted poppy, cover the slopes ; but wherever the numerous springs afford irrigation, the land is painfully terraced for paddy, many embanked fields of this prime necessity being hardly larger than a Soochow bath-tub. We here bought dumplings of glutinous rice, the interior garnished with poppy-seeds. The villages were small, filthy, and ruinous, the people abjectly poor and apparently steeped in opium : our coolies all smoked opium and declared they could not carry loads up these terrible paths without its stimulus. Possibly! as things then were. But a paternal government that should improve the roads and absolutely prohibit the noxious drug might see a hardy race develop such as we find the Miaotse,—deep-chested, rosy-cheeked, and, though men and women carrying heavy loads up the steepest mountain paths, yet free from the curse which is ruining the Chinese. The latter are pale and sickly-looking, but being united, whereas the Miao-tse and Man-tse, split up into independent tribes, have no cohesion, continue to drive the latter back into the most inaccessible and barren regions in the surrounding mountains.

The valley we had been ascending came to a sudden and romantic termination, on the tenth day out from Sui-fu, at the village of Chu-shui-tung or "Issuewater Cavern," so named from its being the site whence issues the source of the Ta-kuan river. Here the white limestone cliffs, between whose walls we had been slowly toiling until we reached an altitude of nearly 5,000 feet, approached to within one hundred yards of each other, when they disappeared under a transverse wall two thousand feet high, smooth-faced, with a rounded, green, grass-grown summit—apparently an insurmountable barrier to further advance. Looking up from the crystal stream gushing forth from the cavern at our feet and being told that our way led up and over this barrier, we experienced the sensation we felt as children when we read of Jack preparing to ascend his beanstalk and mount into regions unknown and bearing all the attraction of novelty. It was a most dramatic scene, apart from the intrinsic beauty of the landscape, and well repaid us for the toil we had endured to reach it. We left behind clusters of sweet-smelling white roses hanging over the foaming stream, birds of many kinds hovering over the face of the water, with beautiful butter-flies among the flowers ; and admired a fresh, wonderful view into the recesses of the precipitous rocks and valleys, as at each turn of the paths the ponies paused to rest and crop grass, their tired feet at each fresh bite threatening to go over the precipice. Another stony zigzag path, hidden in low verdure,—a couple of hours' steady climbing and lo !—we reach the summit of the ridge and find ourselves suddenly trans-ferred to an absolutely new land,—as different from that we had left behind us as though we had crossed the Mediterranean from Africa to Europe. We were at last on the Yunnan plateau. The ridge is known as the " Lohan Ling " or " Arahat " Pass.

We had now left Szechuan behind and found ourselves crossing a level plain bordered by rugged limestone ranges on the right and left, the plain averaging from one to two miles in width. The scene reminded us of a valley in the west of Ireland,—level bog-land enclosed by mountains,— and a cold, drizzly rain, with the mountain summits enclosed in mist, completed the illusion. The path lost itself in the moor, and suddenly, much to the alarm of our Szechuan coolies, we found ourselves crossing a quaking bog, from which we only extricated ourselves coated with black peaty mud. The bog was covered with a weed then in flower,—a rich mauve blossom which gave the plain the appearance of being under crop, but neither dwellings nor cultivated land were visible, making the wildness of the scene very impressive. It was dark when we arrived at the small village of Wu-tsai or "Five stockades," where the usual odours were smothered in the sweet smell of burning peat which is here used for fuel and which, with the accompaniment of excellent potatoes for supper, completed the illusion of having suddenly reached the Emerald Isle. At this point a small

clear stream, coming from the valley to the
south, falls into a rock chasm on the west side
of the plain, and is said to be the true source of
the Ta-kuan or Lao-wa-t'an river, the stream
reappearing again at the foot of the Arahat
Pass.   It would seem therefore that the romantic
hollow bounded by this ridge is probably
a " sink " on a grand scale, such as is common in
limestone regions.   The villagers also pointed out
a dyke which runs through the plain and which
they stated was the remains of an attempted
canal to drain the marsh, begun by a late Fu-tai
of the province, with intent to carry the water
over and down the pass, but after spending some
myriads of taels the work had been stopped for
want of funds and so the plain remained the wild
marsh we have described.   We continued our
journey up the valley by a level earth road,
where we were at last able to have enjoyment
in riding our ponies, the road passing between
hedges white with May blossom and the hill-
sides covered with rhododendron and azalea
bushes, now in full flower, the blossoms of the
former being especially fine specimens.   We
had constantly to ford the wide shallow stream

c

meandering over a pebbly bed, through grassy country with scattered scrub and small trees and patches of cultivation along the foot-hills. In the little village where we halted for tiffin on the second day out from Chu-shui-tung, we bought a fine Reeves pheasant for 100 cash (3 pence) then ascending to the water-parting—a ridge which closes in the valley on the south, to a height of 7,500 feet. Here is the alleged true source of the Lao-wa-t'an river, the drainage on the other side being into the Chao-tung plain which we now entered.

It was pleasant riding through the uplands, and down the earth road by a gradual descent, past grand graves with lofty stone pillars in front of them, between hedges red with roses, pink with roses, among tangles of sweet flowers. There were also many small plantations of bush-like trees for breeding wax insects, cypresses trimmed up and looking very handsome; with also a pleasing view of distant hills across the wide valley. But we were tired out before we arrived at the end of the thirty miles we had set ourselves to do that day.

The prefectural city of Chao-tung is a walled town of 30,000 inhabitants, built in the midst of a dry but fertile plain of considerable extent, being some ten miles wide and about twenty miles long (N. by S). The city stands about 7,000 feet above sea-level and the plain is surrounded by rugged mountains which rise from one to two thousand feet higher. The soil of the plain is the same yellowish limestone detritus, which yields excellent natural roads, drying up immediately after rain and only swampy where the traffic of centuries has worn the road down into hollows, in which the water collects and forms veritable quagmires for the toiling pack coolies and pack ponies to struggle through. Here, however, the greater part of the local traffic is carried on by primitive bullock carts. The valley produces large crops of maize, poppy, oats, barley, buckwheat, and potatoes, besides rice along the banks of the many small streams that descend from the surrounding hills and go to unite in the Chao-tung river below. A pleasing and homelike appearance is contributed to the scene by numerous flocks of sheep and herds of cattle and ponies as well as of swine, grazing on

the hill-sides, the want of which in the ranges
bordering the lower Yangtse valley gives to these
latter such a bare and unfriendly appearance.
Chao-tung boasts a flourishing establishment—
teaching and medical,—of the Bible Christian
Mission, and we much enjoyed here the hospitality so freely offered by our inland missionaries
to passing travellers, and the meeting with cul-
tured people who, unlike the Chinese, upon whom
one is so largely thrown for social intercourse
in these remote parts, have a soul above the all-
absorbing interest of " cash." We left Chao-tung
for the journey of five stages south to Tung-chuan,
with a north-east gale blowing and cold rain
falling,—fortunately at our backs,—the thermometer marking 55.   Upon reaching the edge
of the plain and entering the foot-hills of the
higher mountains to the west we passed over
slopes of brick-red earth (much like the red
laterite along the Yangtse near Kiukiang),
intermixed with pebbles ;   ancient lake beds
filling the hollows in which black peat marshes
alternated with irrigated paddy-fields.   Farms
of thatched adobe occupied the slopes of these
" bottoms," picturesquely ensconced in groves

of Scotch fir, fine large walnut, apricot, and
ligustrum lucidum trees. These latter, a kind
of privet, are grown to breed the wax insect upon,
prior to his transportation to Szechuan. The air
was sweet with the scent of roses, while beneath
the trees the grass was often white with
anemones, but the extraordinary number of great
yellow hips on the hedges was perhaps the most
striking feature.

Huge cubical blocks of a shaley limestone lay scattered in many of the bottoms,
and we passed several abandoned coal adits and
iron-mines, the latter traceable by the vast
masses of slag thrown out by the workmen of old.
The strata hereabouts appeared mainly horizon-
tal, whereas farther south we were struck by
the sight of limestone mountains, the strata
in which had been tilted to the vertical. We
ascended to 8,000 feet to cross the pass of
Ta-shui-ching or " Great Spring," from the
summit of which issues a fine stream of clear cold
water whose course we now followed down by a
break-neck descent to the valley of the Niu-lan
river, four thousand feet below. The view
from the summit of the pass extended over

ridge upon ridge of steep rugged mountains as far as the eye could reach, and, it being a fine, clear day, we sat long and enjoyed the view, while our coolies took a well-deserved rest in the grove which overshadowed the gushing water. Around us were bracken and pines, strawberries with fruit already reddening, limestone rocks pointing up through the earth, like so many sharp teeth. We slept on the banks of the Niu-lan river in the village of Kiang-ti: which we found uncomfortably close and smelly after the mid-day temperature of 51 degrees at Ta-shui-ching. Kiang-ti, which means "River bottom," is a dirty one-street village, squeezed in between the almost vertical cliffs and the river-bed : the river itself is a raging yellow-ochre torrent about 100 feet wide, which here rushes on its way to the Kin-sha at a level of 2,000 feet below and thirty miles distant. The river is crossed by a handsome suspension bridge, decorated with supporters of lions and monkeys cut life size in solid bronze. These bridges are a great feature along the main routes of travel and without them during a great part of the year travel would be impossible ; pity that

By Mrs. Archibald Little.

Kiang-ti Bridge across the Niu-lan, decorated with Bronze Monkeys.

To face p. 38.

the same attention has not been paid to the upkeep of the roads which they connect!

We delayed our start the next morning in order to give time for the path to dry after the heavy rainfall of the previous night; yet our coolies had a hard struggle notwithstanding—we were over two hours doing the first three miles—to carry us up the ravine formed by a side torrent which falls into the Niu-lan, and up whose bed the path now led. At times we forded the torrent; at times crossed by substantial bridges remarkable for the variegated-coloured limestone blocks of which they were built. An ascent to 7,000 feet brought us to the "Summit Notch" (Ya-kou-tang) from which we descended into a remarkable "Pa-tse" or Flat, characteristic of the region. Tsung-kai or "Central market" consists of a perfectly flat level-bottom land walled in by steep mountains, the feet of which, in places vertical cliffs, dip under the present plain. The old lake bed, whose waters once opened a way out through a gorge to the south, by which it was eventually drained, is un-mistakable. The fertility of the soil was shown in the well-built, tiled farm-houses,

surrounded by extensive fields of paddy, then
just ready for planting out, and the groves of
fruit trees with which the " Pa-tse " was studded.
Blackberries, raspberries, and strawberries all
but ripe, an extraordinary provision of berries
of all kinds, now gladdened the road, together
with huge forget-me-nots, and very velvety
flowers of the different brilliant hues of the
Zinnia ; but the previous descent from the
Summit Notch had been like a garden laid out
in coloured sands and not yet planted, the mountain sides, red, yellow, and slate-coloured, bare
of trees, shrubs, and even grass in long stretches,
and worked by water into what looked like
crowds of men massed together. We could not
help thinking what eerie work it must be climbing
these mountains by moonlight, when the shadows
would give the men the effect of moving. But
probably no one moves after nightfall in these
regions.

Our road now led on for five days up and down,
through similar diversified country, across ridges
7,000 and 8,000 feet high, barren limestone mountains with intervening small fertile plains ; all old
lake basins, well cultivated with comfortable

farms embowered in groves of firs, cypress, and
fruit trees. Occasionally we crossed the dry beds
of lakes, which are flooded as the rains increase
in volume, but which were then level, brown earth,
affording good going for man and beast. Some
of the lakelets ("hai-tse" or seas they are called
in Yunnan) were already filled with yellow
water; some, we were told, are perennial; the
"wet" lakes we had to circumvent by long
détours along the edges of the surrounding
mountains; some of the "dry" ones, which
we were able to cross in a straight line, had
rocky islets covered with coniferæ projecting
from their floor and reminding us of similar islets
rising from the sea in the sheltered bays of the
Japanese Inland Sea : many of the "hai-tse"
were still unreclaimed marsh, and the absence
of inhabitants led us almost to fancy we were
exploring a new world. A wild hai-tse of this
description, many tens of miles in extent, lies
at the foot of the Chin-niu-shan or Golden
Calf mountain, a high range in the distance
on our right, away in the direction of the
Kin-sha.

The mountains we passed over were deeply

scored by dry ravines, brick-red gashes in the
green slopes which we had often to make long
détours to head off. At the extreme points
of such ravines, a fragile bridge of a few sticks
of fir branches covered with earth, formed the
path. These gashes would seem to originate in
cloudbursts which carry off the surface detritus
and expose the bed rock below : this was exposed in the shape of pyramids of hard limestone,
from the size of a sugar-loaf to that of a small
church steeple. In many places on the mountain
sides, where the strata appeared to be tilted
vertical, parallel rows of such pyramids gave a
striking appearance to the landscape. The
mountain slopes are mostly barren and uninhabited, contrasting wonderfully with the
fertility of the valleys, but their flanks are
sometimes covered with thick forests of coniferæ,
the green foliage forming a striking complement
to the red soil in which it grows. At the top
of one pass, Lung-shui-ching, there was a delicious
spring of cold water, from which it takes its
name, also a most beautiful cluster of orchids
growing in the fork of a fine maple, and in full
blossom, but too high up for examination. Few

of the ravines, gashed as we have described, showed actual traces of water, the dry thirsty soil being very absorbent, and we can only quote cloudbursts, or as Chinese say, " Chu Chiao," the " Eruption of a Dragon," to account for their existence. At times our way led through narrow valleys, along the path of a purling str am mostly tree-lined, with rich fields and good farmhouses, when the sudden ascent of a wall barrier at the top of the valley would take us into wild uninhabited country. At length, on the first of June, we crossed the last of the interminable passes separating Chao-tung from Tungchuan by a Ya-kou or " Notch " rising to nearly 9,000 feet, and the vale of Tung-chuan-fu lay 1000 feet below us.

Chao-tung-fu, as we have seen, lies in a wide, open plain : Tung-chuan-fu, the second and last city passed after leaving Ta-kuan-t'ing on the way to Yunnan-fu, lies, on the other hand, on the north side of a steep range of mountains, hemming in the old lake basin, which forms the centre of the prefecture, on the south. From the top of the gap, or notch, we looked down on the flat " Hai-tse " ; here, some three miles

wide, and with a glass could just distinguish the
walls of the city at the foot of the opposite range,
which looked green and well-watered. The
steep slope we had now to descend to reach this
" bottom " was covered with knobs of limestone
of all shapes and sizes, projecting from the red
soil, and produced the effect of a huge graveyard
adorned with rows of tombstones ; some stones,
however, appearing like goblins, gnomes, people,
antediluvian animals, or teeth, and the general
effect very uncanny. The scanty herbage afforded pasture to flocks of goats, herds of swine,
and not a few sore-backed pack-ponies turned
out to regain condition. Our own ponies from
Szechuan were as fresh as paint and seemed
thoroughly to relish the cool bracing air, and
greatly to enjoy being ridden again, after their
experience of being led up and down the awful
paths of the Lao-wa-t'an valley--a nightmare upon
which we ourselves looked back with delight at
our escape as we now rode freely over the dry
earth roads of Yunnan. On reaching the bottom
we found ourselves upon the edge of paddy-
fields, the rice being grown right up to the
limestone rock ; across these our way led to the

city, where we were to repose a couple of days before going further.

The plain, or more correctly, "hai-tse," of Tung-chuan we found to be still in part un-drained marsh; it and the paddy-fields, reclaimed from it, being intersected by drainage canals flowing between high tree-planted dykes, with a practicable pathway, about 18 inches wide, along the top. The high road traversing the valley thus meanders between paddy-fields and swamps, the remains of the old "hai-tse" or lake, until the city walls, erected on the high ground, are reached. These drainage canals provide water intercommunication to the small villages nestling on their banks, and we noticed many scows conveying loads of peat to the back doors of the houses. The population were all busily occupied planting out the young rice in the flooded fields, this work here, as generally in Yunnan, being performed by women; and it was pitiful to see them stumping about in the slush with their tightly-bound, mutilated feet; yet they were singing at their work, happy to earn sixty iron cash per day, for what is eminently skilled labour.

We were again hospitably entertained here
by the Bible Christian Mission, and here, as in
Chao-tung, opportunity of our visit was taken
to hold anti-footbinding meetings, overflowing
meetings which were attended by many of the
officials and notabilities of the place. Tung-
chuan is a poor mountain city with not half the
population of Chao-tung and, notwithstanding
the rich valley in which it stands, the population
has a poverty-stricken aspect, especially in the
surrounding villages, while in the city itself
we did not notice any good shops, and were told
there was not one for the sale of silk, whereas
in Szechuan silk is an article of dress common
to all but the very poorest. Our missionary
friends informed us that all the good land was
owned by a few rich gentry, ex-officials, who
reside within the city walls and extort half the
crop from the wretched farmers for rent.   There
were once very productive copper mines in the
neighbourhood, but these, being under official
management, were no longer flourishing.   The
Government provides the funds, but the Mining
Commissioner and Treasurer of the province
were said to be over half-a-million taels in arrear

and only then furnishing about 500 tons of copper annually to Peking. All the copper mined in the district having to be delivered to Peking at a fixed rate—considerably under the current market value of the metal—the weiyuan, or deputies in charge, feather their nests by selling a portion of the output surreptitiously at its full value. I have often asked—seeing that all the copper mined has to be sold to Peking— Whence comes the supply for the coppersmiths for which Yunnan is famous, copper incense-burners and bronzes generally being in evidence everywhere throughout the province? An official will reply : " There are wicked men who melt down the copper cash as we coin it." But it is really impossible to discover the truth about anything in this topsy-turvy country, as all Chinese-speaking foreign residents know to their cost. We found the climate of Tung-chuan quite wintry, a cold rain falling during our forty-six hours' stay, and we could have done well with a fire indoors,—much as often at the same season of the year in country places in England.

We started again from Tung-chuan on a lovely summer's morning—the air bright and fresh

after the late rains—passing through the city
and out at the west gate at 9 a.m. Unlike
Szechuan, where business commences at daylight,
the shops there were then only just beginning
to take down their shutters, and one meets few
of the opium-smoking citizens moving about
in the streets before noon. Thus we never
saw the good brass work for which Tung-
chuan is famous, nor had any opportunity
for investing in the red felt, the best of
which is made there. A new red felt cloak
on a horseman often adds a very picturesque
touch to a Yunnan landscape.

The path at first led west towards a steep range,
about 2,000 feet above the valley, and then turned
sharp south up a side ravine, down which flowed
a swift, muddy river, 80 yards wide and 3 or 4
feet deep, the path pleasantly sheltered from the
now hot sun by many large trees. We passed
large stacks of firewood from the mountains
piled along the river bank for conveyance in the
flat-bottomed boats of the city. The narrow
valley was well cultivated with paddy and
maize, water being drawn off from the river
into side irrigating channels and the river itself

Outside a Yunnan Town.

Solitary Horseman, his bedding folded over his saddle.

To face p. 48.

being endyked in places with solid stone embankments. Where the river impinged upon the valley walls, forming cliffs, these had, as usual, to be surmounted by steep up-and-down paths, which our ponies, now accustomed to the rough foothold, negotiated without difficulty. The hill slopes exhibited patches of purple shale alternating with jointed limestone. At one point in the valley, a river of clear water gushed forth from under the rock-wall, and thus we had the spectacle of two rivers flowing down the same valley, each on its own side, one of clear and one of muddy water. We continued to follow up the muddy stream to its source near the village of Shao-pai (Patrol Station). Here the valley came to an abrupt termination, being walled across by a steep mountain barrier, reminding us, on a small scale, of the great barrier at Chu-shui-tung, up which we had made our first great step on to the Yunnan plateau. We now suddenly climbed another 1,500 feet and ascended a second step which brought us to a higher plateau of about 10,000 feet altitude. Originally a broad stone road, in zigzag, had been built up this barrier ; but now the bulk of the

D

paving had been washed away and a steep,
slippery path alongside, upon which it was
not easy to keep one's footing, had been trodden
out of the steep hillside and formed the only
means of access to the summit.

The plateau, when we at length reached it,
exhibited a patchwork of brick-red and dingy
green, disintegrating limestone with patches of
coarse grass, and appeared uncultivated and uninhabited, but the hard, dry, sandy track
made good riding. This new upland was by no
means level, but consisted of rounded hill-tops,
with higher ranges in the distance on either side,
to east and west, our course being always
steadily south. We descended from the high
plateau to a level some 500 feet below, by the
wide, pebbly bed of a stream, into a more cultivable country, though still the same barren-
looking red soil : but here the level lands were
being sown in wide fields of potato and buckwheat. The ground was being ploughed by
oxen, and as the furrow was opened out, a
boy followed with a sack of seed, already mixed
with a dry, powdery manure of burnt dung and
earth, which he carried over his shoulder and

which he deposited in the furrow, seed and manure together, by means of a wooden shoot
attached to the sack which he carried on his
shoulder. The Chinese could not afford our
more liberal method of a preliminary manuring
of the whole field to be cultivated, and hence,
when not adopting the system just described,
dibble a spoonful of the precious stimulant
separately in the hollow assigned to each group
of seedlings. On the hill slopes were flourishing
fir plantations and comfortable-looking adobe
farms.

The country now, on our third day out
from Tung-chuan, became more rugged and less
plateau-like ; we rounded numerous tarns, some
full, some dry, some large enough to deserve the
Chinese appellation of hai-tse, and everywhere
we found the land ploughed and crops in seed
wherever cultivation was practicable, although
we saw few inhabitants, and only at very
wide intervals came across small villages of ten
or a dozen cottages. At a place called Yeh-
chu-t'ang (Wild Boar Hall) we left the high
plateau, here 9,500 feet, to descend into a valley
1,800 feet below, bounded on our right (west)

by a steep range of mountains sloping abruptly
down to a narrow river valley, fine forests covering the lower slopes. The path on our side of
the valley descended a slope nearly as steep, and
led through woods exhibiting countless varieties
of conifers as well as deciduous trees ; the same
red soil of limestone detritus yielding a dry path
notwithstanding the torrential rains through
which we had to keep on our way. The scenery
here was very fine, the clouds rolling along the
mountain tops as we rapidly descended.

It was already darkening in as we reached the
little mountain village of Siao-lung-t'an (Small
Dragon Fountain : t'an having apparently that
meaning throughout Yunnan), and we put up in
a rough but clean earthwalled inn. The Dragon
Fountain turned out to be a reality as well
as a name, being a fine stream of beautifully
clear water which gushes forth from under
a limestone rock at the head of a wooded glen
above and supplies the village below with
water. We had seen much goitre as we came
along and it seemed especially prevalent in lovely
Siao-lung-t'an ; this the villagers attributed to
the fallen leaves from the trees overhanging the

stream, these decaying made the water unwhole-
some if drunk unboiled. Why they did not
adopt the obvious remedy of removing the
dead leaves which lined the bed of the sparkling
stream, remained unexplained. We ourselves
found the water delicious and preferred it unboiled. In our descent from Wild Boar Hall
we had met with neither houses nor inhabitants,
and now we found Dragon Fount village
consisted only of twenty-six cottages and one
large brand-new Buddhist temple. The north-
east wind and rain increased during the night
and we found our shelter uncomfortably cold
and leaky, having some trouble to shift our
travelling beds into dry spots, but the fresh,
sweet air reconciled us to any amount of
discomfort when we thought of our friends in
Chungking, stewing wearily in the still, hothouse
atmosphere which distinguishes the Upper
Yangtse Valley at this season. Yet we had
not bargained for two days' stay at the
Dragon Fountain; but the incessant rain led
us to give ear to our coolie headmen, as they
protested that the quagmires would be impassable and the streams dangerous to ford.

Prepared for summer travel, we shivered in a temperature of 53 maximum, with a keen wind blowing. At length, on the third morning, we made a start and descended by a steep path of loose stones floating in red mud, through fine woods of walnut and fir trees, to a rolling country, more like our idea of a plateau than any we had yet traversed.

It continued raining for some distance, but this did not prevent the birds from singing. Since we had left Tung-chuan the songs of the birds had been our great refreshment. Birds are very numerous in Yunnan, and as there seem to be no sportsmen there they are quite fearless. We crossed ridge after ridge of low hills, the vivid green of the fresh grass making a fine setting for the dark pine forests ; altogether we saw more timber in this region than in any part of China hitherto visited. Constant streams from the neighbouring heights provided irrigation for extensive paddy cultivation in the little dells and flat valley bottoms, the slopes of such basins being covered with young crops of buckwheat, red pepper, the oil-seed plant, potatoes, and maize.

The soil was here more shaley and varied
through all the shades from yellow ochre to deep
purple, but the outcrop of bare limestone pinnacles and nodules was still noticeable in all
directions ; innumerable such blocks were worn
by what looked like the potholes cut out of the
similar formation in the Yangtse Gorges by the
action of water and of the gneiss boulders brought
down and worked in the potholes by the summer
freshets. But, as one cannot imagine the whole
Yunnan table-land to have ever been subjected
to a similar torrential washing, it is evident that
these circular openings are here due to the con-
cretionary nature of the limestone, out of which
nodules have been worn in the course of time
by atmospheric weathering. The vast extent of
the limestone formation in West China is very
remarkable : it spreads from the western border
of the alluvial plain of Hupeh—which is first
met with some fifty miles east of Ichang—right
across the two provinces of Szechuan and Yunnan till the snow-capped mountains that run
north and south along the Tibetan border are
encountered, where igneous rocks first come to
the surface. This statement, however, has to be

accepted with some qualifications. The limestone below Ichang passes under the Hupeh
alluvium but crops up again in isolated ranges,
all round Hankow and east as far as Wusueh,
where it reappears in the high range cut through
by the Yangtse in the pass of "Split Hill."
Again, there is one (and only one) notable in-
trusion of igneous rocks in the limestone expanse
described, viz., in the section of gneiss and por-
phyry exposed by the Yangtse in the broken
mountain-range that intervenes between the
Ichang and Niu-kan Gorges. In Eastern Szechuan
—in the "red basin" proper—the limestone is
largely overlaid by the new red sandstone, which
has filled in all the hollows between the parallel
ridges of limestone mountains, that still raise
their heads above it. In Yunnan the remarkable feature is the great height to which the limestone expanse has been raised since its original
deposit under the waters of the sea, and the
amount of folding, besides denudation, to which
it has been subsequently exposed.

We continued through similar dry, wooded,
red-earth, rolling country until, on our sixth day
out from Tung-chuan, we reached the first town

on the route, the large, dirty, and apparently prosperous settlement of Yang-kai (Willow Market). Here, June 10, we found a fine two-storied inn with a central courtyard 100 feet square, then a sea of black-green slush which had to be crossed on stepping-stones; the place farther boasted two likin stations. On the previous day we had come across a busy likin station in the village of Kung-shan, the courteous superintendent of which informed us that his collection amounted to the large sum of 10,000 copper cash daily; there the passing coolie and farmer had to pay a few cash on every basket-load. At Yang-kai the superintendent informed me that his collection amounted to Tls. 30 per month only, just sufficient, as he said, to meet the expenses of the staff of four men employed in the office. Anyhow, our man-servant had here to pay 75 cents on two pieces of Szechuan silk he was carrying to Yunnan-fu to trade with, having neglected the precaution he had adopted at the dreaded likin station of Lao-wa-t'an, of hiding the silk amongst our luggage, which the likin officials were good enough never to search. We had passed a file of Hua Miao-tse, so called

from their " flowery " or parti-coloured petticoats,
coming into Kung-shan, whom we should have
liked to have examined and photographed, but on
catching sight of us, as we rounded a corner on our
ponies, the timid creatures bolted up the hill as
fast as they could run—and they run uphill like
deer—nor could their shyness, as we had also
found with the Man-tse in Szechuan, be overcome
by the, generally in China, all-powerful " cash,"
for which indeed they have no use.

On the seventh day we descended (the ground
now sloping steadily to the south, until the
Tonking frontier is reached) into another
ancient lake basin, now a level expanse, some five
by ten miles, surrounded by an amphitheatre of
mountains. The bulk of this area was then trans-
formed into rice fields; the population there likewise being all occupied in planting out the young
rice-shoots: a portion of the plain was still un-
drained mere, intersected by narrow clear water
channels by which small, shallow boats were taking
peat to the villages, scattered amidst the swamp
fields. Part of the road by which we had descended was actually thirty feet wide, a charming
country lane between banks covered with wild

flowers and lined with fine trees ; but now the highway across the plain had narrowed to thirty inches and less, and we had a difficulty to keep our footing on the slippery narrow mud paths which meandered amongst the paddy-fields.

There is little doubt that in the "good old days" China was traversed by practicable roads, well kept up ; but under the present Manchu dynasty, —never truly at ease on their usurped throne, and so discountenancing everything tending to free gatherings of the people,—these fine roads of inter-communication—canals and highways,— have been allowed to go to ruin, while the officials, who have paid dearly for their posts and are uncertain of their tenure, will not move a hand or spend a cash in attempts to restore them.

On the far edge of the plain we ascended a rise to the town of Yang-lin (Willow Grove), a busy crowded place,with well-paved streets, good inns, and a population of 1,500 families.   Command-ing the high road to Szechuan, Yang-lin was long a bone of contention between the contending forces at the time of the great Mahomedan re-bellion, finally suppressed just thirty years ago. No trace of the desolation of that period is now

visible in Yang-lin, and, as an outpost of the
capital, from which it is distant thirty miles,
it enjoys considerable importance. The town
stands 7,000 feet above sea-level, being 500 feet
higher than Yunnan-fu. Leaving Yang-lin, a
wide paved road leads across undulating moorland country, and in places through thick forest,
amidst the shelter of which we halted for tiffin,
warming ourselves and drying our wet clothes
at a blazing log fire on the floor of a woodman's
cottage. Thence across a broken country, a
very garden of limestone pinnacles, "island"
hills, crags and serrated ridges, to the walled
village of Ta-pan-ch'iao, situated in a small
rich "haitse" of paddy-fields. The depression
of Ta-pan-ch'iao is left by a long ascent through
wooded country, leading up to a "ya-k'ou" or
notch, from the summit of which our eyes were
rejoiced with a glimpse of the famous Sea of
Yunnan, our present destination, and the longed-
for termination of our arduous journey.

The view from the "notch" beyond Ta-pan-
ch'iao was very fine, another wide prospect of
mountains with the thin silvery streak of the
lake, here looking like a river, thrown in. The

Lofty Stone Column, such as are common
in Yunnan, and recall Cornish Crosses.
Near Chao-tung-fu.

By M. Monnier.

Primitive Bullock Cart, axle revolving with wheels,
whining sharply as it does so. Outside Mêng-tse.

To face p. 60.

far western horizon was bounded by the cliff-like wall of the Hsi-shan, the range that shuts in the lake to the west, its cliffs falling vertically into the waters at its feet. The plain of Yunnan and the pagodas and walls of the city were hidden from view : another ridge had to be surmounted before we were able to look down on the city itself and its setting of bright green paddy-fields.

PART II

YUNNAN-FU

June 12—August 21

A S is the case with all Chinese mountain cities,
the capital of Yunnan enjoys a most picturesque situation. Emerging from the plain it stands
on a limestone ridge, along which its north wall
runs; the southern wall encloses much flat
land, including a considerable extent of paddy-
fields and lotus ponds, across which run stone
causeways leading to temples and tea-houses;
a bit of Japan with Chinese dirt and decay
thrown in. The view over the city and the
distant lake and the amphitheatre of surrounding mountains is very beautiful, as one takes a
seat on one of the rugged limestone rocks, that
cover the face of the slope of the ridge inside
the north wall. Like Peking and Chĕngtu, the
city is full of fine trees, amidst which glitter
the variegated tiled roofs of the many temples

and guildhalls. The eye reaches across the city,
with its very elegant twin pagodas marking the
spot where the Burmese tribute bearers used to
assemble—the stable for their elephants was near
the British Consulate, where a new school was
being built—and across the wide lake to the
mountains beyond : these distant mountains
form the water-parting between the valley of the
Yangtse, to which the drainage of the Yunnan
Lake basin belongs, and the drainage of the lakes
in the east of the province which goes to feed the
West River of Canton. At this season the cloud
effects are very fine ; showers are constantly
proceeding at some portion of the circumference,
and, night after night, the sunset was preceded
by a rainbow in the east. A walk through the
city is not so pleasing : the streets are narrow
and the shops extraordinarily small and necess-
arily accommodating a very limited stock of
goods ; they are more like booths at a fair, but
built of adobe bricks, with roofs too low for me
to stand upright under ; the population looks
well-dressed and well-fed, although the men
appear to spend their time mostly in smoking
cigars out of inordinately long bamboo pipes,—

and a foreigner in the streets attracts no notice whatever.

I had pictured Yunnan-fu as a sort of Geneva, with a beautiful lake washing its quays; but here is another disillusion;—unless you ascend an eminence you see no lake at all; its shores are five miles distant from the city walls and you have to cross five miles of intervening paddy-fields to reach it : to do this occupies about three hours in the big clumsy sampans which carry on communication with the lake ports by means of the deep winding creeks that intersect the marshy plain, at whose north-east corner the city is built. The water may originally have come up to the walls, for the lake is now receding, as the monsoon rains bring down yearly countless tons of detritus, and new land is being constantly endyked and reclaimed by the industrious Chinese. The marsh has been persistently drained by canals, the high embankments of which, planted with trees, are a pleasing feature in the landscape. By these creeks firewood, stone, lime, and vege-table produce are brought right up to the city gates from the mountainous western shore, and the refuse carried off. Outside the South Gate,

in what was then a desolate region, mostly
covered with ruins of the mud-walled houses of
the country, the ground was being laid out for
the new French railway station;—and this
quarter, at that time still in ruins from the late
Civil War, promised to be ere long the centre of
a large population and of the activity attending
the railway terminus of a great trunk line. We
knew that the railway had been authorised, but
we were not a little surprised to see the works on
the embankment, and on the station, in full
swing, and a large yamên as the residence of the
" Chef de Section " and his staff,—some twenty
Frenchmen all told.

The whole line from Lao-kai to Yunnan, a
distance of about 300 miles, had been let out in lots
to contractors who tendered for the work. These
" entrepreneurs " were mostly Italians, who had
had experience of similar work in Eastern
Europe and Africa, and who employed Chinese
labourers at the rate of $1 each every four days.
There were said to be altogether 1,000 Italians
and 10,000 coolies then (1904) at work on the
line. Everything in these parts appeared to be
going on smoothly, but below Mêng-tse, where

E

the ascent is made from the Red River valley
to the plateau (a rise of some 3,000 feet), the
line being carried up by the valley of an affluent
of the Red River, called the Nam-ti, difficulties
had arisen and the work there was temporarily
at a standstill. This was in consequence of the
deadly malaria, due to what the Chinese call
the Chang-ch'i, or poisonous air, which seems
to infest all the descents from the Yunnan
plateau to the valleys at its feet, especially on its
southern and western borders. In the summer
all employed, Italians and natives, appear to
have been seized with the malaria and to have
had to quit the valley, large numbers having suc-
cumbed to this fatal fever. Henceforward probably work in the Nam-ti valley will only be
carried on in the winter. Notwithstanding these
inevitable delays the French superintendents
were confident of having trains running to
Yunnan-fu in four years' time. In accordance
with their contract with the railway company,
the Government of Indo-China were under
penalty to complete the line through French
territory in 1905, i.e., from Hanoi to Lao-kai,
by which time the cuttings and embankments

between Lao-kai and Yunnan-fu would be ready
to receive their rails and material. The revolu-
tion that the accomplishment of this boldly-
conceived work will effect in stagnant Yunnan
is inconceivable,—besides the boon conferred
upon the European residents of the surrounding
tropical regions by making this unrivalled
sanatorium accessible by steam to the outer
world.

For the most remarkable feature of this
province of Yunnan is its climate, which is,
I should say, the most equable in the world.
The capital is situated at the medium altitude
of 6,500 feet above sea-level and in latitude 25
north. Here, in June and July, we have been
enjoying delightful spring weather—warm sunshine and cooling showers with the heaviest
rainfall always taking place at night; the air
being at the same time fresh and pure and dry,
the average day maximum being 75°, and night
minimum 65°. In winter there is perpetual
sunshine, and a range, as we noted from the record
of the past two years kept in the French hospital,
of only about ten degrees lower, so fires are
seldom needed. The biting north-west winds

which make eastern China north of the Yangtse
a purgatory during their spell, are unknown in
Yunnan, notwithstanding its high altitude. The
prevailing winds in winter, as we saw from the
register above-mentioned, are south-east and
south-west : in summer, short spells of north-
east winds are common and these bring rain and
cool weather. In short, you can live in Yunnan-fu
with open doors and windows all the year round
as in the tropics, and enjoy the fresh air minus
the tropical heat and damp. No wonder that
a recent French traveller, after languishing in
the steamy heat of Indo-China, writes :—" Le
Yunnan doit être considéré comme le prolonge-
ment économique necessaire de notre Indo-
Chine, sa citadelle aussi et son sanatorium, son
grenier de ravitaillement en blé, orge, bétail,
moutons, chevaux, et en général toutes produc-
tions des climats tempérés, sans perdre de vue
le vaste domaine minier offert à notre activité."
Yunnan is the third largest province in the
Empire, and has an area of 108,000 square miles.
Compare Great Britain, 88,000 square miles.

All thanks are due to the enterprise of the
French Government in opening up this splendid

country to the world : Tonking, acquired by
the French at about the same time as Upper
Burma by ourselves, has been pacified later ;
but, no sooner were the Black Flags and the
pirates on the Red River cleared away than the
construction of a railway into the jungles north
of Hanoi was taken in hand : while we have
been talking the French have been acting. Our
Indian Government commenced a railway, which
was to "tap" Western Yunnan, in a half-
hearted way, and then stopped short one hundred
miles from the Yunnan frontier ; and so the
Mandalay-Kunlong line now runs one hundred
and seventeen miles north-east of Mandalay,
and there ends in the jungle and has, of course,
little or no traffic. The French railway to
Yunnan-fu will cost about five millions sterling,
and it will doubtless, for many years, be depend-
ent upon the Government subsidy for a dividend
—but the cost of this subsidy will be amply
repaid by the indirect advantages which the
railway will confer upon the French possessions
in Indo-China. A similar guarantee from the
Indian Government would enable the connection
of Burma with the western capital of Yunnan,—

Ta-li-fu, to be effected, and the guaranteed interest would be amply repaid in the indirect advantages to British trade : for the cotton-goods and hardware that Yunnan requires from abroad can be more cheaply supplied from Rangoon than from Tonking. But it is as a sanatorium that Yunnan will prove of the greatest value to the European inhabitants of the surrounding countries,—Indo-China, South China proper, Siam, and Burma. The wastage of European lives in all these countries is very great and, of course, means a great pecuniary loss. With Yunnan accessible by railway, an epochal change in the conditions of life in these adjoining tropical countries will be brought about ; and we should take our share in rendering this change available to Indo-Burma by a short cut from British territory, even at some pecuniary sacrifice.

Another point which I had read much of before actually visiting Yunnan was the want of population. But certainly, in the country through which we passed, there was no derelict land : every furlong available was under cultivation, with dry or wet crops according to the nature of the soil, while large tracts of moorland, such as in England would be given over to gorse and bracken, were under the plough. Railways and the opening of mines, provided the officials are ever seriously compelled to welcome foreign mining instead of as now endeavouring to obstruct it by every device they can put forward, will develop new industries, and so provide for a larger population than Yunnan under present conditions can possibly support. Should the contemplated occupation of eastern Yunnan by the French be carried into effect, the people, as distinguished from the officials, would undoubtedly be the gainers, and, with the present cordial relations between our two Governments, it ought not to be impossible to agree upon terms mutually beneficial to the trade of our respective countries. That some such eventuality was the original meaning of the Hanoi-Yunnan railway cannot be doubted.

The Confucian temple within the city is exceptionally grand, the dignity of the images in many of the other temples, together with the serenity of their expression, very impressive, whilst the environs of Yunnan-fu teem with interesting

antiquities. The traces of the great Mahomedan
rebellion are to be seen all around the city in
temporary forts and trenches, bearing witness
to the bitterness of the struggle which lasted
for twenty years (1855-1873). It had its origin
in a secret decree sent out by an imbecile
Governor to all the prefects of the province
to massacre the whole of the Mahomedan
population in a single night ; —another St. Bar-
tholomew, which, though only partially carried
out, drove the then utterly unprepared Mahomedans to rebel in self-defence. The rebellion
was ultimately suppressed with the aid of foreign
breech-loading guns, which the Mahomedans
were powerless to resist, and culminated in the
terrible massacre of the whole population of
Ta-li-fu, after the city had surrendered upon the
promise given by the then notorious Governor,
Tsên Yü-ying (the father of the present Viceroy
of the two Kwang, Tsên Chûn-hsuen), that the
lives of the inhabitants should be spared. All
this history is well described in the fascinating
account of the rebellion given in Rocher's
standard work. To-day the Mahomedans of
Yunnan form the most energetic and civilised

portion of the population, being clean in their habits and not addicted to the vices that are undermining the stamina of the purely Chinese population,—who are mostly from Szechuan and the other neighbouring provinces.

According to the R.C. priest who had lived in Yunnan-fu since before Margary's murder, Tsên Yü-ying, towards the end of his life, used to be carried about in a sedan chair, with incense burning underneath, and all the people prostrating themselves and adoring as he passed along, temples being built in his honour even in his lifetime. He had so many heads cut off that in the end—haunted by phantom heads, heads everywhere begging for life—he would put to death one after another of the officials accompanying him, till one by one all fled. At last, returning from Ta-li-fu, he shut himself up mad, and in a fortnight was dead, as was believed, by his own hand. Then the people destroyed the magnificent sepulchres of the Tsên family, about five miles outside the west gate.

But whether all this is true we had not time to investigate, any more than to examine the Lolo village hard by the spot. These villages seem always to be a little off the direct road; the men like gypsies, with pale, thin faces, and felt hats with high brims in front, crushed down behind; some of the women wearing a curious hood, with three points in front.

During our stay in Yunnan-fu we made various excursions to the picturesque mountains which encircle the basin in which lies the city with its great lake, a fine sheet of water 23 miles N. by S. and 12 miles across at its greatest width. On the western shore the mountains (there about 1,500 feet) dip steeply into the lake, the waters of which, when we first crossed it, were covered with lilies so frail and tiny as to produce the effect of white foam studding the water. A zigzag, well-paved road led up to a group of temples situated over half-way up, the road being cut through a forest of fine large fir trees—the absence of the usual bare mountain slopes being due to the presence of the temples. These temples are invariably surrounded by extensive groves, proving what a valuable resource in timber the Chinese neglect by their thriftless annual burning of the mountain slopes in the dry season—besides the calamities of alternate

floods and drought for which they have only
themselves to thank. Here the priests, in olden
time, had cut out a gallery in the face of the
cliff and had left *in situ* pillars and ornamental
balustrades excavated in the original rock, at
a point whence there is a sheer drop to the deep
water below, and from which there is a magnificent prospect across the lake to the picturesque
city of Yunnan and its amphitheatre of mountains
to the north and west. There is a fresh, airy
room with stone images on the walls, and a round
stone table in the middle, all cut out of the rock,
and there were light, airy half gateways along
the gallery; the other, inner half being solid rock,
and the rock overarching cut into the semblance
of fantastic windows, with towards the end light
pillars, resembling Ionic columns in their grace
and simplicity, with clouds carved in stone at the
top. Behind in the rock is a dragon in high
relief, a spring of deliciously cold water proceeding from its mouth, a frog in relief looking up
at it, and a fat frog altogether cut out, looking
up across the roadway, another dragon in slighter
relief opposite. There are many other such
fancies, but nothing appealed to us so much as

a very fine lion of grand proportions lying among some ruins, half hidden by shrubs, beside the landing-place. The site of our tiffin on the terrace in front of the temple was truly unique, and the air, then in mid-August, was fresh and cool, though the direct rays of the sun in this latitude (25° N.) are always hot.

Crossing the mountain at the north end of the lake, we came upon a village inhabited entirely by Lolo, tame Lolo as the Chinese call them, in contradistinction to the sêng or raw " Lolo, who have not yet fallen into line and taken on Chinese civilisation. The tame Lolo wear Chinese dress ; they are generally smaller, athletically built, and far more lively than the Chinese proper, who in Yunnan are mostly the descendants of immigrants from the neighbouring provinces of Szech-uan and Kweichow. Whether owing to the fact that they cannot stand the altitude and so take to opium smoking as a relief, the fact remains that the Yunnanese are, of all Chinese, the most illiterate and the most apathetic, and are certainly not equal in energy to the aboriginal Lolo and Miao-tse, whom they so cordially despise.

In the range to the N.E. of the city is a remarkable mountain with twin peaks, known as the Tieh-ling, or Iron Mountain, sacred to Fêng-shui, with a temple surrounded by a fine grove at its foot. The limestone strata are here tilted to the vertical, and the consequence is that, from a distance, the mountain has a striped appearance. As we climbed the steep sides of its peaks, which rise some 800 feet above the average of the range, we found these stripes resolve themselves into ridges of harder stone, broken up into more or less isolated blocks of rugged weathered limestone, while between the ridges were depressions, where the softer intervening strata had been denuded. These are now all grass-grown and afford pasturage to mobs of ponies, as well as to cattle and swine. The lines of black rock and the intervening strips of grass give the mountain its striped appearance and, in the eyes of the Chinese, its sacred character. The story goes that the Tieh-ling forms the head of a dragon, whose tail is in Szechuan, and hence that he devours the riches of Yunnan to cast them forth again in the favoured province to the north.

Another charming spot in the same range,

ten miles east of the city, is Hei-lung-t'an, Black
Dragon Spring, where is also a fine temple
guarding a stream of pure water which gushes
from the limestone and afterwards goes to form
a small river; the meandering course of the
stream being traceable, as it winds across the
rice plain, by the triple row of fine old fir trees,
originally planted on the slopes of its embankments. This, its principal affluent, falls into
the lake opposite the Hsishan. The hill sides
are here covered with a fine variety of deciduous
trees, bamboos, and coniferæ, the property of the
temple. The city itself, being built on the slope
of a small limestone ridge rising out of the plain,
which disappears under the expanse of paddy-
fields intervening between its walls and the lake,
forms a prominent feature in the landscape.
This ridge, scattered over with picturesquely
shaped protruding limestone blocks, both outside
and inside the city wall which runs along its
crest, falls to the south in fantastic cliffs, yielding
caves adorned with ancient inscriptions, while
handsome temple pavilions, reminding us of
Peking by their architecture and spacious courts,
are built on the level ground below. Beyond

is the Lotus Lake, which, with stone causeways
running through it, leading to pavilions, tea-
houses, and paddy-fields, is all enclosed within
the city walls. Here too is the provincial
arsenal, employing some two hundred men,
the workman superintendent being then a
Shanghai man once in the employ of Farnham,
Boyd & Co. The nominal head was a Taotai
from Hunan (Mŏ), who commanded a division
of Hunan braves in the inglorious Chinese cam-
paign in Manchuria in 1894.

The city of Yunnan successfully withstood
three sieges during the Mahomedan war of 1856-
1872, the last siege having been raised as the
place was about to surrender, owing to the
hitherto successful Mahomedan General Ma Ju-
lung, having surrendered to, some say having
been bought over by, the Imperialists at the
moment when final victory was within his
grasp. This defection of his best general
rendered hopeless the cause of the Panthay chief
at Ta-li-fu, and gradually the rebellion was suppressed and the country "pacified" by the
ruthless Governor Tsên Yü-ying, in the final
massacre of the inhabitants after its peaceful

surrender in January, 1873. Ma Ju-lung's timely
surrender saved Yunnan-fu from a like fate, and
the desolation within its walls that still char-
acterises all the other towns of the province with
few exceptions. A life-like statue of the famous
Futai has been erected in a spacious temple built
in his honour. Dressed in his official robes,
his painted features show a striking family
likeness to his hardly less famous son, one time
Governor of Shansi, afterwards Viceroy of
Szechuan, and then Governor-General of the
two Kwang provinces.

The extensive suburbs had not yet recovered
from the total destruction to which they were
subjected during these successive sieges, notwithstanding that the last took place over a generation back. The new French railway station,
the buildings for the staff, and the proposed
foreign concession, were being erected amidst
the ruins of the south suburb. Apart from the
railroad staff of some twenty Frenchmen located
in this suburb, the city then contained, of foreign
residents, a British and a French Consul-General,
two China Inland missionaries with their families
(rosy-cheeked children, testifying to the healthy

Viceroy Tsên Chûn-hsüan with his two little Sons.

This likeness was presented to Mrs. Little by the Viceroy himself on the occasion of her audience about Foot-binding.

To face p. 80.

climate), a French postmaster, and a French army surgeon, who had charge of a hospital erected for the benefit of the Chinese inhabitants by the French Government, which also grants the services of the surgeon, paid by the French Goverment. By the time the railway is completed, Yunnan will doubtless be made a " Treaty Port," as is the case with Chi-nan-fu, in Shantung ; when cheap and rapid communication with the coast will afford opportunity for the establishment of foreign merchants, as a considerable trade is certain to be done, provided only that the present onerous transit dues through Tonking be removed or modified by the French Administration of that otherwise progressive colony.   As it is, hundreds of laden pack animals now pass daily between Yunnan-fu and the head of navigation on the Red River.

As to the Yunnan plateau itself, we have already shown how different we found it to be as compared with our previous expectations.   We had imagined a comparatively level, in parts rolling, upland, similar to our experience of the Mongolian plateau and the highland to the north of Sung-pan—we found it a sea of broken,

F

rugged mountains varied by a succession of
rich oases, the product of now reclaimed lake
bottoms. We had yet to traverse the country
between Yunnan-fu and Tonking, along the
line of the railway which was being pushed
forward with such energy through a very difficult and, as we were told, an extremely picturesque country, but before doing so, whilst
all our journey hither was still fresh in my
memory, I thought it well to write an account
of what we had so far experienced in this extraordinarily interesting corner of the vast Chinese
empire.

PART III

FROM YUNNAN-FU TO LAO-KAI

Aug. 25—Sept. 15

THERE are two routes open to the traveller desirous of escaping from the remote capital of Yunnan to the outside world and the civilisation of the West—both arduous and difficult, both leading over high mountain passes and by deep river valleys—the one due west to the valley of the Irrawaddy, across the defiles of the Mekong and the Salween, and so on to Rangoon—the other due south to the valley of the Red River and thence to the coast at Haiphong, the seaport of French Tonking. If bound to Europe, the road to Rangoon is the more direct, and by much the shorter : returning to China, we chose the way by the Red River rather than traverse once again the terrible pathways of Lao-wa-t'an and northern Yunnan ; notwithstanding that the latter leads across the

healthy uplands of the northern plateau, while
the southern route dips down to the low encased
valley of the Red River, which has at this season
a bad reputation for heat and malaria, and by
which we found the discomforts of travel far
greater than those on the land journey. On
the other hand Haiphong could be reached from
Yunnan-fu in about a fortnight, while the journey
overland to Sui-fu—where the Yangtse is reached
and the luxurious travel on the Great River is
resumed—would occupy a full month's time.

In leaving Yunnan for the coast, we diverged
from the direct road to Mêng-tse in order to
learn somewhat of the progress of the railway then
building : so, instead of proceeding due south
and following along the east shore of the Yunnan
lake, we turned off almost due east across the
mountains to the city of Y-liang, the seat of the
headquarters staff of the northern section of the
road. The " tracet " or alignment of the railway
had been a sore subject of discussion and had
been twice changed ; the question being : Should
the line follow the old Chinese trade route to
Mêng-tse and Man-hao, thus taking in the principal
cities and tapping the more populous valleys of

the region ; or should the alignment be the easiest obtainable from a technical point of view ? Both presented great engineering difficulties, involving heavy outlay for cuttings and tunnels, so that it is not surprising that the engineers should have finally decided on taking the line round by defiles which nature had excavated, although the country passed through is mostly without population or trade.

The Yunnan plateau, as we have before stated, is nothing but an endless succession of small isolated oases—cuvettes or basins—some filled with deep-water lakes, others partially occupied by shallow meres,—dotted about amidst a sea of rugged mountains. These basins, where alone the Chinese staff of life, paddy, is cultivable, are naturally the only abodes of population, who communicate with each other by passes over the walls of their respective basins ; the few small rivers that flow above ground have cut out deep narrow defiles in the limestone and have provided no surplus room for villages or agriculture, while their gorges form a practically impassable barrier to inter-communication. The main problem, therefore, before the Yunnan Railway Company,

was how best to climb the wall-like ascent of
5,000 feet from the Red River valley on to the
plateau ; whether to ascend by a natural gorge
and so proceed in the direction of least resistance,
but through a wild, unpeopled country, or
whether to follow the old road and so pass from
basin to basin either over the intervening
mountains or beneath them. This latter was
the plan originally selected, but, after much time
and money had been spent on the survey and
some preliminary work had been executed, it
was ultimately determined to follow up the
defile of an affluent which rises on the high
plateau to the east of Mêng-tse, and 2,000 feet
above that town, and thence falls into the Red
River at Lao-kai. North of Mêng-tse and between
it and Yunnan-fu, the line now determined upon
follows up the comparatively easy valley of the
Ta-chêng-kiang up to the "basin" in which
stands the city of Y-liang, leaving the high road
from Mêng-tse to Yunnan, from which it is
separated by a lofty mountain range, some 30
miles to the west. After traversing Y-liang
the railway turns west, winds through another
deep gorge and then, crossing a low pass (500'),

at length emerges in the Yunnan plain. The
total distance from Lao-kai to Yunnan-fu by the
new " tracet " is 448.2 kilometres (=280 miles),
which is six kilometres longer than by the old
" tracet." This is the work to be carried out by
the Yunnan Railway Co., who will eventually
have the exploitation of the whole line from
Haiphong to Yunnan-fu, a distance of 521 miles,
in their hands, for which a loan of £4,000,000
has been guaranteed at $3\frac{1}{2}$ per cent. interest by
the French Government. From Hanoi to Lao-kai,
a distance of 311 miles, the railway, which follows
up the left bank of the Red River, is being built by
the Public Works Department, *i.e.*, by the
Government of French Indo-China, and this line
the department is under penalty to the Yunnan
Company to complete by April of 1905. At the
moment the line was only in working order as
far as Viétry, 225 kilometres short of Lao-kai ;
the line had been laid up to Yen-bay, 82 kilometres farther, but on this section the embankments along the river had been washed away by
the summer freshets. When trains are running
through the whole 521 miles from Haiphong to
Yunnan-fu, as it is expected they will be three

years hence, the Yunnan sanatorium with its
dry bracing air may well take precedence of
Japan as the health resort of Tonking and South
China.

We reached Y-liang on the second day out from
Yunnan-fu, passing along the "chemin de service,"
a " cornice " road, cut by the railroad men, which
skirts the mountains to the north of the Yang-
tsung-hai, a charming mountain lake, about 12 by
2 miles, which the French call " Petite Suisse,"
and where it was in contemplation to open a
station and build a summer hotel when the line
is completed. The scenery thereabouts was very
pleasing, the mountains being wooded and
abounding in orchids, which we picked as we
went along, especially one like a white bird
with wings dispread, six inches across, and with
a tail as long in comparison as that of a Reeves
pheasant. The good Father Maire at Yunnan-fu
seemed to think it new to Europe. Chinese
habitations are conspicuous by their absence,
and the whole country has the charm of a
region newly opened to travel. The little lake is
entirely enclosed by mountains and its waters
are deep blue. We descended to the ford of the

small river which drains the lake eastwards and
which joins the Y-liang basin by a deep gorge,
of which the engineers have taken advantage to
run the railway through it. All gorges in
limestone country have a family likeness, and
this one might be the Wushan Gorge of the
Yangtse on a small scale, with its cliffs rising
vertically from the water's edge, capped by steep
mountain slopes above. The gorge is some ten
miles long, while the river, that has cut it out, is
barely twenty yards in width : it flows with a
fierce current, the city of Y-liang lying nearly
1000 feet below the level of Yunnan-fu. The
roar of the stream and the boom of the explosions
where the tunnels, of which there are sixteen in
this one defile, are being blasted out, was audible
on the *chemin de service*, which is cut at a level
some six hundred feet above the water, the
mountain peaks rising nearly 1000 feet higher.

The first night we slept in a temple, which the
railway company had cleared out and built on
to for their staff. There were no tables nor chairs,
and our servants were for the first time at fault
and could suggest no substitutes for these in-
variable concomitants in every Chinese inn.

Our only companion in the building was a Greek from Egypt, only arrived that morning from Tonking, until a poor fellow was borne into the courtyard on a litter and lay there groaning terribly, his face and chest all blackened, he having been blown up with fifty pounds of gunpowder two days beforehand. His friends were conveying him to the capital, which we had just left, in hopes of there finding some medical assistance. The unhappy man's groans forced home the terrible need there is of doctors and surgeons in China.

Our stage on the second day (26th August) was Y-liang, but shortly before sunset we were caught in the heaviest thunderstorm it has ever been my fortune to be out in ; the road became a quagmire, and as the day darkened in we came to a full stop within some four miles only of our destination ; the flashes of lightning showed a village ahead, to which we painfully made our way, and took refuge in an empty outhouse : our carrying coolies failed to put in an appearance, and we went supperless to bed, sleeping on the floor, and only learnt next morning that this house had been built to rest coffins in, as also to offer a refuge to houseless vagabonds—like ourselves. This is the second time only, in years of travel, that we experienced such a *contretemps* and had to pass a night without our bedding, but it was actually impossible for the heavily-laden carrying coolies, having once dropped behind, to come on in such weather in the dark ; they had found shelter some two miles to the rear, and were very apologetic when they joined us at Y-liang on the following day. Fortunately the weather was mild, and we suffered nothing worse than a night's discomfort.

The Hsien or district city of Y-liang is a small but busy place built on the edge of a rich " pa-tse," through which flows the Y-liang river on its way to join the Ta-chêng, which ultimately finds its way through Kwangsi province into the China Sea. Here we found a French colony of railway people—thirty-five foreigners living in a pretty little enclosure all to themselves—and from them we received every kindness, Mr. Prudhomme, the superintendent, together with his hospitable consort, regaling us with a true Parisian dinner.

At Y-liang we left the line of the railway and,
turning west, crossed the range of mountains
that separates the valley utilised by the railway
from that through which passes the main road
to Mêng-tse. Our object was to visit the big
lake of Chên-kiang, which, lying in a fold of
these mountains, aloof from any of the main
thoroughfares, had been little visited by Europeans, excepting by those engaged in surveying
the country with a view to laying out the
railway. We took two days from Y-liang to
reach the city of Chên-kiang, from which the
lake takes its name, and which is built at its
northern end ; although, measured on the map,
the distance between the two cities is within
twenty-five miles. But we had to cross the
two walls of an intervening basin—the
Tsaopu "hai-tse"—a flat about five miles by
one and a half, with the remnant of the old
mere filling up its northern end—ascending
on one side 1,200 feet, and on the other 2,800
feet above Y-liang to do so. The little village
of Tsao-tien, in the midst of the hai-tse, is charm-
ingly situated in a grove of trees surrounded
by fields of paddy, maize, tobacco, and sun-

flowers ; grass and furze-covered moorland leading up to the mountain slopes, which are, as is
most usually the case, bare of trees and uncultivated. On the way, there were beautiful orchids,
and, as when approaching Y-liang, mostly white
flowers, but besides these a pretty little geranium,
the flower white with pink centre, growing
downwards from the stem, so that one could never
see it and the leaves at the same time ; there
was also a strange blue flower, all blue feathery
stamens, calyx and corolla almost invisible.
Blackcaps were singing very sweetly, but for
Yunnan there were few birds in this part.
We spent here our first night out from Y-liang
in a primitive but clean inn, having come only
sixty li.

After crossing the ridge, on the following
morning, we descended through a wooded valley
with small clearings of buckwheat, but with no
houses or population visible, until we came to
the foot of a steep cultivated mountain on our
right hand, rising about 3,000 feet above the
valley. This conspicuous mountain dominates
the northern shore of the large Chên-kiang
lake, the prefectural city of Chên-kiang being

built on a " flat " between it and the great
lake. Fifteen miles out from Tsao-tien we tiffined
in the outskirts of the small village of Niu-chuang
(cattle depot) in a grove of acacia, palm, pine,
willow trees, and bamboo, in which we sought
shelter from a heavy shower. We had now
risen to 1,900 feet above Y-liang, and there
was a delicious freshness in the air and a cold
autumnal feeling, although we were still in the
month of August. There were few birds, but
lanes with hedges composed of all sorts of plants,
and on the way down many azaleas, also the
curious blue flowers again, and very large yellow
evening primroses. A steep descent of twelve
hundred feet for a distance of six miles, through
broken country and by paths of red shale,
afforded grand views over the mountain-
embosomed lake (in size and appearance com-
parable to the Lake of Lucerne, but minus the
snow peaks in the background), and brought
us to the walled city of Chên-kiang. Chên-kiang,
though a walled city and looming large on the
map, covers less ground than does the district
city of Y-liang; its area is about half a square
mile, and—most exceptional in China—it has

no suburbs without the walls : it is built
on the northern edge of a strip of level paddy-
fields which, similarly to Yunnan-fu, separate
its walls from the deep water of the lake, this
cultivated strip being about a mile in depth and
extending a distance of three to four miles along
the northern shore of the lake. The city is
traversed by wide but dirty streets, and we
failed to find any tolerable resting-place within
its walls, so, after a long search, ultimately
secured rooms in a horse inn outside the south
gate, sleeping over a malodorous stable crowded
with galled ponies, where all night through,

> " Champing golden grain the coursers stood
> Hard by their pack-loads, waiting for the dawn."

We left Chên-kiang by a path coasting the
lake, the waters of which a strong south wind
was dashing in breakers on a pebbly beach, with
not a single sail to break the water horizon
glittering in bright sunshine : the poorly-found
lake boats (and, such as they are, there are very
few of them) only venturing out when the wind
falls after sunset. After three miles thus following the north shore, we turned south and proceeded by a path which runs up and down

along the foothills of the mountains dividing
the lake basin from that, through which runs
the high road to Mêng-tse, and which rise immediately from the lake shore. We passed one
or two small villages where a narrow flat allowed
of rice cultivation, until, towards evening, we
approached a conspicuous cliff-sided limestone
peak, some fifteen hundred feet in height, known
as the "Chien-shan." Yesterday we had
thought it like the Sphinx, to-day like the
Matterhorn. Here we ascended steeply eight
hundred feet, the path leading past the top of
a smooth, straight slope of detritus, newly fallen
from the cliffs above, to a "col" created by
a precipitous limestone cape, which here juts
out into the lake, and from the crest of which
we enjoyed a fine view over the lake, and the
dimly perceived higher mountains that bound
its eastern shore. A rapid descent on the other
side led us into a small, enclosed valley filled with
paddy-fields, but without a house visible: thence
over a second "col" similar to the preceding,
—the point enclosing a small, snug boat harbour,
—into another terraced valley running back
between wooded precipitous mountains, the

rice-fields following up the mountain stream almost to its source. Here we found the little village of Lu-tsung ("Midway"), where we put up for the night.

We left Lu-tsung by a path still continuing along the shore, occasionally rising over projecting headlands affording lovely views over the lake,—having close on our right a steep, rugged, cloud-capped range which divides the basin of Chen-kiang from that of Kiang-chuan,— a range rising to about twenty-five hundred feet above the lake. The lake is a dark blue colour, and probably very deep,—a true mountain rift. In this showery weather the farther shore was generally invisible, and, with the waves breaking on the clean boulder beach, close along the edge of which the path now led, we seemed to be coasting a sea shore. Again, to-day, not a sail was visible, the lake, although twenty-two miles long, being of little use to the natives as a channel of communication. Along our narrow trail we met a few teams of pack ponies carrying cotton yarn from Mêng-tse and the Red River, but the traffic here is very small compared with that between Mêng-tse and Yunnan-fu.

G

Shortly after passing Mi-shin, a village situated
five or six miles above the southern or lower
end of the lake, the country opens out, and the
hills there, being composed of softer material
as compared with the hard mountain limestone
of the road so far traversed, have been washed
down, and a comparatively easy road across
the water-parting is thus available into the
valley of Kiang-chuan. A wide break in the
mountains had been formed, leaving a comparatively large area open to cultivation, which
here as elsewhere was chiefly devoted to paddy.
The divide between the two basins, which may
rise to five hundred feet, is formed of shales,
including a tough whitey-grey marl, which has
been denuded into terraces and cliffs, and
possibly the strangest rock shapes we had yet
seen—Lot's wife, clasping her knees; a cathedral;
every sort of fantastic shape. We descended
on the west side into the basin filled by the
Nan-kwang lake (so called locally), at the upper
end of which is situated the walled city of
Kiang-chuan. Though a hsien or district city,
Kiang-chuan measures only about a quarter of a
mile each way, and seems to contain little else

than an imposing three-storied drum tower, built
at the intersection of its main north and south
and east and west streets,—the distance from
Lu-tsung, whence we had set out in the morning,
being about fifteen miles.

Our destination for the night was, however,
the village of Hai-mên-ch'iao, ten miles to the
south as the crow flies.

The road, after leaving this little town, was
especially pleasing, with magnificent trees by the
side, also a row of very handsome graves; then,
two columns with little laughing lions on top,
and fine laughing lions sitting underneath,
and graves again. And again, beyond the
graves, the little Nan-kwang lake smiling in
the sunshine, as seen through acacia trees; a
crescent chasm of red rock at the top of the cliff
to our left, and, as if fallen out of it, sitting at
the bottom, a red stone frog.

The road was bad, at first winding through
paddy-fields and then leading up and down over
the out-jutting promontories of the Nan-kwang
lake. The naturally poor road was made worse
by the continuous rains, but we were reconciled to
the attendant discomfort by our arrival at Hai-

mên-ch'iao,and its attendant interests. The meaning of the name is Sea-gate Bridge, and the village
is reached by a picturesque three-arched stone
bridge, beside a quaint two-storied house; the
bridge crosses a narrow river by which the
Nan-kwang lake drains into the lake of Chen-
kiang. This river, which is little over ten
yards broad at its narrowest, and is about a
mile in length, flows with a swift, deep current
past limestone cliffs on its left bank, to its outfall
opposite a small, high, wooded island situated
near the southern extremity of the larger lake.
The small river would seem to have cut out a
gap for itself little wider than its actual bed,
leaving, along its right bank, room for a path,
along which we walked, shaded by fine banyan
trees, to take our farewell view of the big lake,
now illumined by the setting sun ; returning
in the dusk, as heavy rain again set in, to find
the main street of Hai-mên-ch'iao flooded, and
our inn door only accessible by wading. We had
now rejoined the high road to Tung-hai and Mêng-
tse, which we quitted, not far from the city of
Yunnan, in order to make a détour by way of the
Y-liang defile and the shores of Lake Chên-kiang.

These twin lakes, as one might well call them, united as they are by a short river which makes its way through this curiously narrow gap in the dividing range, are the third and fourth in the series of the five lakes that lie to the south of Yunnan-fu, and which make such an attractive feature on the road thence to Mêng-tse; the great Chên-kiang lake being the third, and the smaller Nan-kwang lake, upon the east shore of which stands the village of Hai-mên-ch'iao, being the fourth. The following morning found us posting along the east shore of this latter lake, which we estimated to measure nine miles north and south by four miles east and west, the surrounding mountains being low, not over 1000 feet. It stands, of course, at nearly the same level as its sister lake, the Chên-kiang, which is about 100 feet below that of the lake of Yunnan-fu, say 6,300 feet above the sea. A noticeable distinction is that the ridge south of the Yunnan lake forms the water-parting between the Yangtse valley drainage and that of the " West " river of Canton, these four lower lakes all draining into the latter. The Nan-kwang lake is pretty but not sublime as is the Chên-kiang lake,—at

least when seen in stormy weather as we saw
it ; its banks are fertile and we passed through
many prosperous villages embosomed in fine
trees and orchards of the Chinese date (so-called) ;
tobacco plantations were also largely in evidence.

We left the lake by a two hundred feet ascent
over barren moorland, grass-covered but gashed
with vermilion red ravines, from which limestone
blocks protruded—the same formation we had
found to pervade the province. This moorland
gives pasture to herds of cattle and goats, but
is bare of all culture. Thence we descended
200 feet to another " patse " or flat, a small
fertile oasis in the midst of which stands the
flourishing but extraordinarily filthy village of
Tien-sze-pa, the heaven-born, an old lake bottom :
then over the enclosing ridge into the valley of
the fifth lake, the Tung-hai or "Eastern Sea."
The Tung-hai lake is more striking than the
Nan-kwang, although rather smaller : the surrounding mountains are higher and descend in
cliffs of crystalline limestone and white marble
to the old lake shore, which now stands a half-
mile or more inland, leaving a richly-cultivated
level border between them and the present lake,

and again giving space for flourishing villages. The weird appearance of the surrounding cliffs must have struck the holy men of old, for temples abound and the mountains behind them are covered with rich forest in consequence. Many of these cliffs are curiously waterworn, and in places overhanging. Turning round and following up the south shore of the lake upon which stands the district city of Tung-hai, we traversed an extensive rice-plain (the rice now beginning to be harvested), two to three miles in width; all land recovered from the lake, the level of which is now several feet lower than it was many millennia ago, when the waters of the lake undermined the present inland cliffs.

Tung-hai-hsien is a fine old walled city, covering little more than a half square mile, with clean, broad streets, lined in parts by elaborately carved, two-storied shop fronts. There are fine carved stone bases, supports for flagstaffs, before the doors of many of the houses, and the two-storied walls of a dark yellow adobe add much to the picturesqueness. There are also handsome entrances to the houses where Chin-tse live, (men who have taken high honours), very fine golden characters above them stating, "This is the humble lodging of ———." Tung-hai is the centre of a flourishing trade in opium, that of Yunnan being famous throughout China for its superior quality,—being more akin to Indian opium, say the smokers, than is the lighter drug of Szechuan. We slept here outside the town in a temple converted into an inn; the inn, as are many in Yunnan, being kept by a native of Szechuan.

We crossed the southern lip of the basin of the Eastern Sea by an ascent of 900 feet, traversed another moorland, and then descended 600 feet by a very rough path composed of a white limestone shale, with frequent minor ascents and descents, into the basin of Chung-ho-pa—"Central River Flat"—a fertile rice plain surrounded by wooded mountains. Thence the path descended rapidly through a thickly-wooded valley, so much wooded indeed that we could have imagined ourselves in Thuringia rather than amongst the usually bare-burnt mountains of China. The glen we were now traversing was indeed very beautiful, full of very fine trees, then rosy and brick-red earth, water ragged, and

terminating in two limestone portals, barely
a hundred yards apart, which opened on to a wide,
well-watered valley, terraced with rice-fields.
We had now effected a net descent of 250 feet
below the level of Tung-hai. The inhabitants of
the picturesque glen through which we had just
passed were mostly disfigured by goitre. They
told us the land was " cold," and that both the
crops and the water were indifferent.

We now descended into the extensive valley
of Kuan-yi, through which flows a swift-running,
wide, shallow, muddy river coming from the
mountains to the west, and spreading out in
many channels over the here level plain. We
crossed its different arms and intervening sand-
banks by a narrow, wooden, pile bridge, 500 yards
long. Then, across a second swift, deep stream
and over a low divide, a slippery clay-shale
path brought us to the walled city, where we
put up for the night, glad to get out of the rain
which had fallen heavily every day since our
departure from Yunnan-fu.

Kuan-yi is a city of ruins. The landlord of
the newly-built spacious inn told us that it was
now only inhabited by 300 families, whereas

before the Mahomedan rebellion it had held
3,000 families. This city was a stronghold of the
Mahomedans, who held the place from 1860 to
1867, when it was finally taken by assault
by the Imperialists and its inhabitants put to the
sword, the Fu-tai rewarding his soldiers by un-
limited licence, as was common in the religious
wars in Europe three centuries earlier. In 1903
Kuan-yi had again the ill-luck to be overrun
by rioters, this time from the neighbouring
prefecture of Lin-ngan. The walls were in ruins,
and we passed out the next morning through the
south gate of the city, of which nothing remained
but the bare brick lining of the ancient archway.

The Kuan-yi basin appears to have been
scooped out of a marly white shale, and so its
surrounding hills are less precipitous ; it is
about six by three miles in extent and its margin
little over 500 feet high. The path up the
lip had been worn into a defile over-arched by
flowering shrubs and trees, down which rushed
a red torrent, in places two feet deep, through
which our coolies had perforce to wade. There
was beautiful vegetation on either side, and
hollowed out trunks of trees from time to time

conveyed water across the road. A butterfly
like a bit of flame fluttered across our path, then
became mixed up with the deep red blossoms
of the Coral tree, and a creeper with a beautiful
red flower.

We had the pleasure of eating our mid-
day meal not in a dirty inn, but under the
shade of fine spreading trees at Lung-shui-kou,
where we also bought our first persimmons
on this journey. There was much woodland
and some pine groves on the slopes of the
mountains bordering the defile, which rise to a
height of about 1000 feet on either side of the
narrow roadway. This "stage" ended at Hsin-
fang, a poor village of adobe houses (common
throughout Yunnan), with flat roofs of clay and
lime, spread upon rafters of fir poles. The
basin of Hsin-fang measures some eight miles
by four, and is filled with terraced paddy-fields.
As we descended the glen which breaks through
the boundary ridge, we had a fine view of lofty
ranges to the south, amidst which scattered
rainstorms were falling ; we had now, after an
endless succession of ascents and descents,
reached a level 1,500 feet below Yunnan-fu, and

the temperature was distinctly milder. We flattered ourselves that we were now steadily descending to the Red River valley, which, at Man-hao, about 400 miles from the sea, stands at an elevation of 600 feet, but the sequel showed us that we had still many long ascents to overcome and we gradually understood why the engineers had abandoned the obvious line along the high road for the unpromising country through which the railway was now being built. We were interested here to meet some of the aborigines, whom the Chinese in these parts call I-jen.

The soil still consisted of a dry-looking, porous, limestone detritus, with projecting cliffs of hard limestone with red and white faces, and the country generally, after leaving the paddy and maize in the bottoms, was unfertile, wild-looking, and in no way picturesque. Over such desolate moorland we crossed, the next day, a plateau-like ridge, rising 450 feet above the valley. Leaving the busy and turbulent prefectural city of Lin-ngan, the headquarters of the tin-mining industry as well as being an important opium mart, on our right, the road, which hitherto had taken us due south, here turned east and

south-east to Mêng-tse, an important centre,
the seat of a branch of the Imperial Maritime
Customs, the residence of a French Consul,
and the headquarters of the Mêng-tse-Lao-kai
section of the new railway. Approaching
Mêng-tse, now two and a half stages distant,
we crossed many wide, substantially built
stone bridges, and came upon patches of
well-paved roadway, the remnants of a once
Imperial highway, now mostly buried under the
accumulated soil borne down by centuries of
rain and wind. In the middle of a magnificent
bridge over one river there was a beautiful
inscription, and in the middle of that a small
figure of the Goddess of Mercy (Kwan-yin),
austere, but beautiful; a little shrine with
twisted columns underneath the figure. Before
that we crossed a bridge with a very lovely roof.
The very wide road was here so strangely laid
out that we crossed it occasionally, but never
kept to it for many minutes, till it descended
a very narrow defile full of pretty flowers. We
halted at Mien-tien, a village almost totally
destroyed in May, 1903, by the Lin-ngan rebels
under Chou-ma-tse (pock-marked Chou), and on

the following day diverged from the main road to Chi-kai, our next stage, in order to visit the famous Yen-tse-tung, or Swallows' Cave.

The Swallows' Cave shows no signs of its existence from the outside. You approach it by a small footpath winding over rolling moorland until a very ordinary-looking Chinese temple is visible in a fold of the hill surrounded by the usual grove. We had difficulty even in finding our way there, but were fortunate in meeting with one or two peasants in the depopulated country, who were able to put us on the right road. We walked into the temple and saw nothing unusual in the courtyard beyond a Chienlung bronze incense burner, dragons climbing round the pillars supporting the roof, fine bronze Kia-hing vases, and two standard shrubs, hibiscus, one yellow blossomed, the other red, both very large-stemmed and somewhat contorted; together with surrounding low temple buildings. But a Taoist priest appeared and led us through a sort of back door, upon entering which one of the most fantastic scenes we had ever witnessed burst upon our view. It reminded us of nothing so forcibly as the built-up grottoes one sees on

By M. Milhe.

Swallows' Cave from Terrace.

By M. Monnier.

Pack Animals, the Freight Trains of Yunnan.

To face p. 110.

the stage in a fairy extravaganza. We had seen before many grottoes and caves such as are common in limestone regions, but nothing equal to this natural phenomenon hidden away in remote Yunnan. We now stood near the top of the grotto and looked down on a swiftly flowing river, about 20 feet wide, which entered the cave from the north on our left and disappeared in the gloom of a side cave on our right, its waters illumined by the sun shining through the trees which surrounded the entrance, 80 feet below where we stood on a narrow terrace near the summit. Another tree hung over the opening to the sky above, thus adding beauty by the cross lights filtering through the green leaves on to the red and swollen river below. A steep staircase cut out of the rock wound round to a flat terrace, thirty feet beneath us,—overlooking the water across an elaborately carved stone balustrade, surmounted by stone lions—a terrace about forty feet square, upon which we afterwards spread our breakfast table, a very fine solid rock column supporting the upper roof to our left. Side caves, also with stone stairs leading to them, and filled with shrines and carved inscriptions, offered numerous fresh points of view, some of the inscriptions being stuck on to stalactites so high up that we wondered what steeplejack had dared to climb up to them. Thus art had combined to enhance nature in an unobtrusive way, making, as it were, a frame for the picture. But the wonderful charm of the grotto lies in its stalactites. These hang in thousands like banners from the roof, wavy, ribbon-shaped, in delicate tints of white, pink, and yellow. No photograph, apart from the difficulty of finding a suitable light, can do justice to the play of colour or even of the light and shade on a sun-lit day such as that on which we were fortunate enough to see it. When the Yunnan sanatorium is opened by rail, this will be one of its chief show places. We may add that the Swallows' Cave does not belie its name. Swallows' nests were offered us for sale, and hundreds of swallows flew in and out of holes in the rocks during the two hours,—which we would, if we could, have prolonged into two days,—while we were feasting our eyes on this magic picture. The river, we may mention, comes to the surface again two miles lower down, and after disappearing again, ultimately reaches the West River of Canton.

Crossing over more grassy "divides," with limestone blocks protruding everywhere as thick as tombstones in a well-filled cemetery, we traversed three more basin-like valleys, all terraced one-third of the way up their sides until, eighteen miles from the Yen-tse-tung, we reached our destination for the night in the small but busy town of Chi-kai. We crossed two rivers on the way, one clear stream flowing over a pebbly bottom to the south, one yellow ochre stream flowing swiftly to the north, both crossed by solidly-built, wide-arched, stone bridges. Chi-kai is situated not far from a high serrated range, 3,000 or 4,000 feet high, running east and west, and so at right angles to the prevailing direction of the mountains in Yunnan. This range, in which are situated the famous Yunnanese tin mines, dominates the Mêng-tse plain, and forms the most conspicuous feature in the view from the town of Mêng-tse, situated at the other extremity of the "basin." The Mêng-tse "hai-tse" measures about twelve miles north and south, by about half that distance east and west, and

H

contains two meres, the remnants of the old lake. The town is situated in the south-east corner at the foot of the mountains which separate it from the Red River valley and which rise about 2,000 feet above the Mêng-tse plain. We crossed the smaller mere on a stone causeway and passed through magnificent fields of maize, the largest I have seen in China, 300 to 500 acres in extent, the grain, now being harvested, growing to a height of ten feet—a tribute to the fertility of the limestone detritus, carefully manured, which forms the soil. Nearing the town, we found the land laid out in paddy-fields, irrigated by the streams from the neighbouring mountains. These mountains are singularly bare of everything but grass, owing to the annual winter firing of the grass whereby all the young trees are destroyed. Their eastern side is now scored by the railway cutting along their flank. This runs at 1000 feet above the plain and nowhere descends to the Mêng-tse level; it enters the basin by a high pass in the s.e. corner after emerging from the head of the Nam-ti canyon.

Mêng-tse is a hsien (district) city, with well-kept

Yen-tse-tung or Swallows' Cave from below.

To face p. 114.

walls and a busy retail trade, but the main activity of the place is now centred in the east suburb, where are situated the offices of the Imperial Maritime Customs, the French Consulate, the extensive buildings in which are housed the local railway staff, a French hotel and three French trading stores, these latter mainly established to supply the needs of the railway people, of whom some sixty Europeans resided in this suburb and in the immediate neighbourhood. Mêng-tse is the lowest town in Yunnan we had yet visited, being situated at only 3,500 feet above sea-level, and the air, after our residence in the higher altitudes of the interior, felt almost uncomfortably warm. The Imperial Maritime Customs at this " open port " possesses a fine compound several acres in extent, in which stand a series of isolated buildings surrounded by trees ; many of these are eucalypti, which the equable climate seems to suit admirably ; planted little over ten years back, they are now large trees, overtopping the native acacias. The buildings are new, the original buildings having been destroyed in a raid by the workmen in the tin mines in 1898, when the Customs staff had to fly for their lives ; the raid being due to a rumour that the French were about to acquire the mines. The Customs collect dues on the goods imported from Tonking for consumption in Yunnan, chiefly cotton yarn, and on the exports, which are chiefly tin and opium ; these dues are, by special agreement with the French, one-third less than those collectable under the fixed tariff,—a small boon to trade more than neutralised by the exorbitant transit tax collected in Tonking itself. Transit passes are issued here at half tariff rates and free goods from all detention at likin stations throughout the province, and the French take good care that these passes are duly honoured. Railway material and all stores for the railroad staff have been imported free of duty and the land required for the roadway had to be provided by the Chinese officials free of cost. As the greater part was valueless mountain land, this was not a serious matter ; only where the road traversed bottom land had rice-fields to be purchased ; the scale for these was ten, twenty, and thirty taels per mow (a seventh of an acre), according to quality.

While in Mêng-tse we received all possible

kindness and information from the French heads
of departments, who kindly arranged an excursion
for us to the celebrated Nam-ti valley, in which
the most difficult work of the whole route was
being executed ; and I must not here miss the
opportunity to express my gratitude for the
kindness and hospitality we enjoyed at the hands
of all concerned in the work. The Nam-ti, as
the French call it, or Nan-hsi as it is called in
Chinese, is a stream which has its source in the
Mêng-tse mountains and which has cut its way
down through a deep narrow canyon to the Red
River. This it enters, now increased to a stream
eighty yards in width, at the frontier town of
Lao-kai, where it is spanned by a wide bridge
connecting the French settlement of Lao-kai
with the Chinese town of Hŏ-kʻou, and over which
the railway passes. The building of the road
was in the hands of a separate construction
company working under the supervision of the
Yunnan Railway Company proper. This construction company had been recently engaged
in railway work in Salonica and the Levant
generally, and their work was let out in sections
to Italian contractors or " *entrepreneurs.*" One

of these, who had his headquarters at Mi-la-ti,
a village situated near the source of the Nam-ti,
at a height of 2,000 feet above Mêng-tse, we set out
to visit. Riding up a steep pathway over broken
rugged country, we reached the embankment
of the line then being cut out along the mountain
side ; the soil is the same as everywhere in
Yunnan—red sandy detritus in which the prim-
eval harder limestone blocks lie buried, and it
was curious, in a spot where a deep excavation
had been dug out and the looser detritus had been
removed, to see the limestone pinnacles left
in situ, awaiting removal by blasting, much as
we saw them washed out and exposed in the
innumerable dry watercourses with which we
found the mountains scored the whole way from
the Szechuan border to the Red River.

Mi-la-ti stands in a charming wooded valley
high up, surrounded by mountain peaks ; here
the hospitable Italian *entrepreneur* invited us
to partake of an excellent *déjeuner* in his im-
provised Chinese house, the office and headquarters of his section staff, after which he
accompanied us to the head of the canyon,
some five miles farther south, where the line

begins its romantic descent of 5,000 feet to the
Red River. The Mi-la-ti plateau, though broken
into ridges, is a comparatively level basin
surrounded by peaks covered with thick forest
containing many fine trees of varied sub-tropical
growth, the few villages being entirely hidden in
foliage. Towards the southern end of this high
basin the Nam-ti river has worn its way deep down
through the soil into the underlying limestone,
in which it has cut out a miniature gorge lined
with vertical cliffs only a few yards apart. As
it approaches the defile leading to the river,
it breaks into falls, and lower down these are
found of sixty and even a hundred feet in height ;
the railway is carried alongside of them, the line
being run by the side of the gorge, piercing
projecting points by over fifty tunnels, the
longest of which extends a distance of 500 yards.
Owing to the valley being practically confined
to the width of the river bed, and to its being
enclosed between high mountains on either
side (*encaissé*), it is so confined and so closely
shut in that, as the tropical lowlands are approached, the air is completely stagnant, and so
unhealthy that all employed in it, as well natives

as Europeans, sooner or later succumb to the malaria, which is here of a deadly kind. The mortality this year had been so great that work was practically suspended,—to be resumed on the return of the cold season, provided sufficient coolies could be found to work there. Nothing will induce the Yunnanese to descend from their plateau nor, *per contra*, will the Annamites leave their tropical rice-swamps for higher levels.

Thus, not only are the natural difficulties of the land almost insuperable, but a still greater stumbling-block is the task of obtaining the requisite labour to overcome them. In truth, the completion of this railway in the wilds will be a lasting tribute to the boldness of its conception, and to the determination and perseverance with which it will have been carried to a successful conclusion. These eighty odd miles through the gorge of the Nam-ti form the crux of the whole undertaking.

Whether it is right to put so much power into the hands of rough men bent on making as much money as they can, is another question. The *entrepreneur* here frankly told us he was a drunken good-for-nothing till he had to do his three years' term of military service, when he learnt to read and write. The others laughed and said " Not much." This man and men like him have the absolutely irresponsible management each of his piece of the road.

After a very pleasant luncheon party we went to see a great wall he had built, and the beginning of a bridge he was making just where the railway enters the Nam-ti valley. The river was very clear and swift there, yet with a weird, uncanny look about it, partly perhaps because it was so shut in that no sunshine ever reached its channel there, partly perhaps because of the numbers of pointed mountain tops all round.

Our hosts told us how they had been working near Paotingfu in 1900, and were among the few who had escaped from the Boxers, one, a very well built fair Italian, relating how he had carried a little girl upon his shoulders for three days, when she could no longer walk, sometimes hiding in rivers, with her still on his shoulders, almost all the time without food.

Parting with regret from our kind host, the Commissioner of Customs, we left Mêng-tse

by the high road over which passes the by no
means inconsiderable trade at present carried on
between French Indo-China and the province
of Yunnan, a trade conveyed entirely by pack-
animals, for whose benefit mainly exist the fine
fields of maize that distinguish all this region.
After traversing the usual narrow path between
paddy-fields we commenced the ascent of a low
pass crowned by an imposing gateway, past
groves of the wide-spreading Wan-nien-ching
(myriad years green)—a tree not unlike the
banyan; a very strong hedge, made of big cactus
with prickly pears in front, blocking the way
before arriving at them. On over a treeless,
grassy upland, after which we descended again
into a wide, well-watered valley terraced in rice-
fields then harvesting. We rose again by a
well paved path skirting another richly-cultivated
and well-wooded valley on our left, until the
paved road disappeared under an accumulation
of soil which the heavy rain, that now began to
fall, soon reduced to a wretched quagmire. From
this time on we saw no more cultivated, or even
inhabited country, barring halting-places for
the pack animals on the mountains, and the

By M. Milhe.

Gateway on Pass leading out of Mêng-tse Plain to Tonking.

To face p. 122.

transhipping stations cleared out of the jungle
that lines the Red River, until we reached the
populous Annamite delta, then three hundred
miles distant. We were still ascending the
southern lip of the Mêng-tse "cuvette" by a
rise of over 3,000 feet, a distance of seven or
eight miles over barren limestone ridges, until
we reached an upland whence the eye extended
over countless peaks and pinnacles,—the summit
of the high range that forms the north shore of
the Red River. This upland was remarkable
from the number of "mamelons" from one
hundred to two hundred feet in height, which
rose from the level surface,—steep cones of
limestone, the formation consisting of strata
lying at an angle of 45 or 50, the slope on one
side, the edges of the strata on the other; but
how denudation has produced such a series of
perfectly shaped cones it is difficult to explain
alone by the relative hardness of the stone of which
they are formed to that of the mother formation.
Crossing this upland, the only flowers on which
were white everlasting, golden rod, and blue lark-
spur, we encountered a high cold wind, which
chilled us to the bone, and were right glad when,

after cautiously feeling our way over the rough descent, an hour after dark we took shelter for the night in a small " horse " inn, a mud hut in the little village of Shui-tien, 2,000 feet below the summit, where we slept under double rugs and Chinese wadded gowns.

We left Shui-tien by a narrow defile with fine mountains on either side and followed down a small stream, which we quitted to suddenly ascend a pass of four hundred feet on our left, whence we looked down direct upon the valley of the Red River. The river itself is too closely shut in its ravine to be visible until quite near, but we were able to see the corresponding high range which bounds its right bank and so knew that we were at last approaching the termination of our long land journey and were on the point of exchanging the vicissitudes of inland travel for the comparative luxury of the water.

The crest of the high range before us formed, in part, the boundary between Tonking and China, the Red River not being the boundary until the French frontier station of Lungpŏ is reached, some fifty kilometres below Man-hao and sixty above Lao-kai; at which point the river

finally crosses the frontier and from thence
onwards flows entirely through French territory
until its embouchure is reached in the Gulf of
Tonking below the port of Haiphong.

These forest-covered mountains must, in
ancient times, have formed an impassable barrier
between Tonking and China, and account for
the marked distinction in race between Annamites
and Chinese. A wide belt of unpopulated
country separates Yunnan as well as Kwangsi
and Kwangtung from the Annamite region.

We now descended some five thousand feet
in about five hours and dropped from a temperate into a tropical climate even more
suddenly than we had risen three months previously from the stagnant valley of the Kin-sha
on to the breezy uplands of Yunnan. As we
turned a corner of the little village of Tao-tao
we really felt as though entering the door of a
hothouse, and the illusion was completed by the
change to the tropical vegetation by which we
were now surrounded. Tao-tao is remarkable as
being the spot at which the trains of pack-mules
and sore-backed ponies pass the night before
descending to the port of Man-hao ; it being

reputed fatal for man or beast to pass the night in that deadly spot. So the men load up their beasts in the early morning, descend to Man-hao and there deliver their packs, receiving their return loads the same day and re-ascending to Tao-tao the same night to sleep. At length, when about eight hundred feet above it and half-way between Tao-tao and Man-hao, we caught our first sight of the famous river, our goal for so many days past,—a narrow ribbon of smooth, oily-looking, pink-red water between steep, green banks, the hills opposite covered with dense tropical jungle and with no signs of cultivation. The river appeared small and insignificant, though its valley is imposing from the height of the steep mountains that form its shores. Only a high bribe will induce a Yunnanese to pass a night there or indeed to descend within a day's journey of the Red River on any terms.

It was extraordinary the stories we heard in Yunnan-fu and Mêng-tse of the deadly air of this valley, and, had we not been old travellers, we should have been persuaded either to put off our journey thither until midwinter or to return by

land the way we had come. The Chinese, with the
exception of the natives who are born and live
in them, seem far more susceptible to malarial
influences than even Europeans are, and it is
a fact that numbers of Szechuan and Yunnan
coolies, who, under the temptation of high pay,
have consented to go to Man-hao, have fallen
sick and died there. Hence nothing would
induce our own servants, who had promised to
accompany us to the end of our land journey,
to go on with us when the time came, and we
were compelled to send them home from Mêng-tse
and from thence on to " do " for ourselves
until we ultimately got on board the " Messageries fluwales " steamer in Laokai.

We put up for the night in a Cantonese inn in
Man-hao, which is a small place built on a narrow
flat along the left bank of the Red River, and
arranged to take passage in a native boat, the
size of a small " wupan," floored with slabs of
tin, to Lao-kai for the sum of thirty dollars.
Man-hao seemed very quiet and still, the business
of the place,—the unloading and reloading of
mules and the transfer of their packs to and from
the boats moored under the bank,—being over

for the day at the time of our arrival shortly before sunset. The one street is composed of Cantonese " hongs " which attend to this business. The air was certainly hot and steamy and between the showers the sun was intensely powerful, but otherwise we noticed no difference in the climate from what we had experienced on similar days at the same season of the year in Chungking. All the same, we were glad to get on board our boat the next morning and be rowed rapidly down stream. The river below Man-hao, the head of junk navigation, runs from one hundred to one hundred and fifty yards in width and flows down to Lao-kai in an almost continuous rapid.

In the first forty miles we traversed fifteen true rapids, similar to those on the Min River above Sui-fu, which, but for our experience on the Yangtse and the adept management of the Chinese boatmen, we might have thought alarming, the water at some of them coming into the boat. The whole way the banks were covered with impenetrable jungle, masses of wild banana and many unknown trees and flowering shrubs, acacias predominating, but all weighed down by an omnipresent creeper, a sort of

convolvulus which gave to the landscape a
monotonous one-shade of bright green, and so
destroyed the variety we had expected to see
in tropical scenery. There were some palms,
some, but few, birds. One looked particularly
beautiful shrined in greenery, of a brilliant
peacock blue, with a big, hooked yellow
beak. The jungle is so thick that no towing
path exists and the upward-bound junks are
slowly propelled by painful poling along the
shore. We made the downward journey to
Lao-kai of about eighty miles in ten hours, but
were told that the upward journey under favourable conditions occupied as many days and,
when, as then, the freshets were on, it took a full
month to get from Lao-kai to Man-hao. The
scenery as we rushed past it, was very pleasing,
owing to the steepness of the wooded foothills
that formed the banks and the picturesque
outline of the lofty jungle-covered mountains
behind them. Each bend in the river, and there
were many such sharp turns, disclosed a new
picture and showed up new peaks in the distance.
We especially noted two jagged, isolated peaks,
one a precipitous cone flat topped, the other

I

mysterious with serrated summit, both with mists floating round them.

At noon we sighted a small clearing in which stands the village of Shin-kai (Newmarket), which seems now to have been abandoned for Man-hao, thirty miles higher up.   Shortly after, we came to the French military frontier station of Lung-po, consisting of a small clearing on the right bank in which stands a white-washed bungalow surrounded by palisades with a few low thatched native cottages to the rear.   At length, at sunset, our boatmen moored alongside a steep muddy bank, while we demanded to be landed in Lao-kai.

Never before in China have I been so non-plussed by a total inability to comprehend a word of the language of our boatmen.   These appeared to be Cantonese by origin, but speaking a dialect, a mixture of Cantonese and Annamite. We shouted " Lao-kai," but they only pointed down river, and so instead of putting up at the hotel, as our host in Man-hao, through whom we had chartered the boat, had told us we should be able to do, there was nothing for it but to unpack our camp-beds and await the dawn.   In the morning it again poured in torrents, and nothing would induce the boatmen to move, and it was not till ten o'clock that the pangs of hunger forced me to climb up the slippery mud-bank and find out where we were. I learnt from a friendly shop-keeper who spoke Chinese, that we were moored off the town of Hŏ-k'ou, which is on the right bank of the Nam-ti, the French town of Lao-kai being on the left bank, a railway bridge over the Nam-ti connecting the two places. Hŏ-k'ou has one long, busy, very muddy street running between retail shops for a mile or more along the left bank of the Red River. My intelligent friend informed me that there was an Imperial Maritime Chinese Customs here with foreigners in the office, and directed me to the " Hai-kwan," consisting of a sort of mat-shed built amidst the jungle on the slope of the hill, where the kindly Commissioner in charge at once permitted and directed our boatmen to proceed to Lao-kai and to moor below the hotel there. Our detention was due to the boat carrying tin and not yet having entered, owing, I supposed, to the rain, although no one could understand the lao-pan's talk sufficiently to make sure. Anyhow, now our troubles were over.

PART IV
THROUGH TONKING TO HONGKONG

Sept. 15—Sept. 27

LAO-KAI presents the same contrast to Hŏ-k'ou, that the Model Settlement does to the Shanghai city; on crossing the railway bridge that now unites the two towns, one passes abruptly from filth and disorder into wide macadamised streets lined with shade trees; clean white bungalows, one and two-storied, a small bund with pontoon wharf—a miniature Point de Galle with the same tropical air and vegetation, but also a close, steamy atmosphere due to its situation in a narrow valley distant 265 miles from the sea. There are few or no Chinese in Lao-kai (it costs them about six shillings a head to enter French territory) and, in the siesta hour, in which we landed, there were apparently no inhabitants. The military are stationed on the right bank and have to cross the rushing river by ferry

132

to come into Lao-kai; the piers of a high bridge, solid circular pillars of brick and stone, were erected some years ago, but the idea of completing the bridge seems to have been abandoned. The chief buildings are the offices of the administration, a spacious Custom-house with godowns attached, the offices of the " Messageries Fluviales," the Post Office and the Hotel Fleury, where we put up, also a roomy military " cercle," pleasantly situated on a bluff overlooking the river, and a bandstand in the central " Square." Towards evening, after an enjoyable *déjeuner* at the hotel, we sat on the verandah listening to a military band, we having happily arrived on band-day, and felt that in crossing the Nam-ti we had re-entered civilisation ; but we pitied the folk whose duties relegate them to this depressing spot, with little to occupy them, no sports, no society, nowhere to go; hemmed in as they are by pathless jungle. There is the excitement of the arrival of the " chaloupe " from Yen-bay, 143 kilometres lower down (ninety miles) from May to October, i.e., during the season of the summer freshets, after which communication is confined to the tedious native junks. Of course the advent of the railway will change the position, but even then Lao-kai, up to the time when the surrounding country shall have been cleared and brought under cultivation, hardly seems to offer any commercial future. Its importance consists in its being the frontier station on the borders of Tonking and China and in its military depot, which serves admirably to encourage the obstructive Chinese officials at the provincial capital to take a complacent view of French enterprises in their province.

We were fortunate in finding a " chaloupe " of the Messageries Fluviales making her slow way up stream on the following day, and by her we forthwith took passage to Yen-bay, a day's journey down river. The " chaloupe " turned out to be a small sternwheeler, heavily laden with cargo and crowded with " relief " soldiers, French and Annamite, very badly kept, extremely dirty, with one saloon on the upper deck but no accommodation for sleeping or washing. The crew, including captain and pilots, were all Annamite and the engineers Cantonese. Upon crossing the frontier and entering Lao-kai we had left China behind ; Hŏ-k'ou has the usual crowded population of all Chinese towns, Lao-kai seemed to have none; the boys in the hotel were all Annamite and appeared to us far below the Chinese in intelligence and willingness to oblige. They mostly speak French; few Europeans in Tonking except the French employed in the administration, who are paid to learn the language, speak Annamite. The language itself has a marked affinity with Cantonese, and any one conversant with the latter should soon pick it up. The steamer was leaving at 6 a.m., and neither on the evening before nor on the morning itself could the hotel proprietor find coolies to take our luggage down to the boat, and but for the kindness of Mr. Shrigardus, the Commissioner of the I.M. Customs, who brought his own Chinese across from Hŏ-k'ou for the purpose, we should have been in evil case.

Lao-kai is the administrative depôt for the troops stationed along the river down to Yen-bay, a distance of ninety-one miles, and our steamer, the Yen-bay, had the task on this trip of furnishing the different garrisons with their supplies for the coming quarter; these consisted mainly of cases of flour from France, packed in tin. The steamer swung round as we reached the different stations and landed her cargo on the bank, which was carried up by the soldiers, French and Annamite. The stations are little more than clearances in the jungle, and now that the Black Flags and pirates that formerly infested the river have all been happily suppressed, the troops have little to do ; anything more monotonous and depressing than the life led in these lonely spots it is difficult to conceive, and it is hardly to be wondered at that opium-smoking is commonly resorted to as a pastime as well as a prophylactic against the prevailing malaria. Our fellow-passengers were mainly non-commissioned officers, either on short leave for a visit to the capital (Hanoi), or else being invalided home ; one of these frankly informed us that he smoked opium regularly and that only those who did so were immune from dysentery and the prevalent jungle fever.

We reached Yen-bay shortly before sunset and went ashore to dine at the hotel, only breakfast being provided on the steamer, on board of which passengers cannot pass the night. We were however again fortunate in finding a connecting

By Mr. Davidson.

Opium Smoking among Coolie class.

To face p. 136.

steamer in port, leaving in the morning for Hanoi,
and by paying $4 extra for a cabin (we had
already paid $55 each for our passage tickets)
were enabled to sleep on board and so be ready
for the early start in the morning. This "chaloupe," the "Chobdo," was a large sternwheeler
that runs all the year round between Yen-bay,
the winter head of navigation, and Hanoi, 115
miles distant; better found than the wretched
Yen-bay and with ample accommodation and con-
veniences, her crew were equally Annamite and her
engineers Cantonese, but she carried in addition
a French purser, to whose civility we were much
indebted. The river banks still looked much
the same, only there were more palms and
bananas, some trees covered with brilliant red
flowers, and some creepers with equally brilliant
yellow flowers. The trees were still drowned in
creepers. At our first place of call there were
soldiers of the Légion Etrangère busy digging a
vegetable garden. They spoke cheerily and
politely, and it was difficult to believe that all
had left "ruined lives" behind them. The
women from Hanoi were now very conspicuous in their huge hats with lacquer crowns,

surmounting cheery, pleasing faces. Mist and
rain prevailed all day.

Yen-bay, as a residence, was hardly more
attractive than Lao-kai. In fact, the latter with
its well-kept roads, abundance of shade trees,
neat tropical bungalows and background of
forest-covered mountains, was very pleasing to
the eye and decidedly picturesque. Yenbay is
a far busier and more populous place, besides
being the then terminus of the Yenbay-Hanoi
railway. The country there is more open, but
as we arrived towards the close of the summer
rains, which were still continuing, the roads were
deep in sticky red mud, and the white-washed
bungalows presented a muddy and dilapidated
appearance ; the main road, by the river, through
the foreign quarter to the railway station, passes
by a long wide street lined with untidy native
shops and dwellings, reminding us of the suburban
native streets at Singapore. The railway to
Hanoi was interrupted from Viétry on, the
embankments having been washed out by the
torrential rains ; the same was the case with the
embankments laid for the extension to Lao-kai.
These follow up the left bank of the river and

have apparently been built by the "Travaux Publics" too near the water at too low a level, and have suffered accordingly from the summer freshets ; trains will thus hardly be running to Lao-kai by April of next year, and a heavy indemnity will be in that case due to the Yunnan Railway Co. by the colony, which has guaranteed to complete the line by that date.*

After a *very* heavy hot night, much disturbed by discharging of cement and other noises, we left Yen-bay the following morning in pouring rain by the "Chobdo" and at 2 p.m. reached the town of Viétry, pleasantly situated at the point of junction of the Rivière Claire with the Red River. As its name implies, the Rivière Claire is a stream of clear water which descends from the limestone ranges on the Yunnan border to the north, and the "Myriad Mountains" of Kwangsi,—whence it flows in a course forming an angle of twenty degrees with that of the turbid Red River coming from the north-west. Its channel at its mouth is 320 yards in width, where it is spanned by a fine bridge which carries the railway. The Rivière Noire, which rises in Yun-

* The colony kept its word.

nan, rises west of and flows a long distance
parallel with the Red River; after turning sharply
north it joins the main stream on the opposite
shore. All these, and indeed the major number
of the streams traversing Tonking, have their
origin in the mountains bordering the great
plateau (Yunnan), and flow in nearly parallel
courses from north to south. Viétry stands at
the head of the delta which we were now entering,
and was already an important commercial centre.
Between Yen-bay and Viétry we called at more
military posts, occupied some by Annamite,
some by French troops of the Légion Etrangère ;
the Annamites form good soldiers, are smart and
well-behaved, and we were told that they give
no trouble and are free from crime and even mis-
demeanours. They wear a becoming uniform of
yellow khaki with putties and flat-topped hats
of plaited bamboo, trimmed with red, and look
far neater and cleaner than their French comrades
with their loose trousers, blue coats, and pith
helmets.

Our glimpse of Viétry was very picturesque
and attractive ; two magnificent banyans shaded
a very pretty shrine, from which a lovely avenue of

overarching acacias, Flamboyantes, led up to the town. There were persimmon and custard apple trees in sight, also more tropical trees, and a little group of loungers staring just as in Italian towns.

At Viétry we left behind the mountains, and a country apparently bare of inhabitants, and entered the densely-peopled rice-delta, a level expanse 5,000 square miles in extent, that forms the kernel of the colony. From here on, but for the banana trees round the villages, we might be traversing the upper reaches of the Huang-pu, although we are never out of sight of distant blue ranges which form a fine background to the vivid green of the paddy-fields, the second crop of which was then maturing. The delta produces two crops of rice : one reaped in May and one in November. The usual endyked banks here line the river, as also the numerous transverse " arroyaux," or creeks, and protect the fields from inundation : this year, however, the embankments had given way and large areas had been inundated. Hanoi, the capital, which is built in a swamp, comparatively even more low-lying than Shanghai, was seriously threatened. Although by the time of our arrival the inundation

had drained off, yet the grand railway bridge,
which carries the line from the right to the left
bank of the Red River, was so near the water
that our "chaloupe" with lowered funnel
could only just scrape through without touching.

Among our fellow-passengers was a padre of
the Missions Etrangères, who superintended a
chrétienté of some 20,000 Christians in the
interior ; he spoke very highly of the Annamite
people and praised their women as being exceedingly well conducted ; this is noteworthy, in
that the Annamite women, unlike their Chinese
sisters, appear to have absolute freedom, and
do most of the business besides hard manual
labour. Although their civilisation came from
China, they refused to accept crippled feet as
a mark of distinction, though they adopted the
Chinese cut in their dress but with more sober
colours, generally brown and black ; indeed
the gaudy, "criard" colours that the Chinese
glory in are totally foreign to the Annamite
taste, except in the state dress of their mandarins.
The hair is worn in a top-knot at the back of the
head, much as in China in the days of the Mings ;
the conspicuous feature is the hat of bamboo

and palm leaves, which with the men is always pointed (as in Kweichow and Yunnan) and with the women flat, as large as a cartwheel and nearly as heavy. Men and women generally go barefoot and their carriage is excellent—a great contrast to the bowed Chinese. As a race they are far more homogeneous than are these latter, the head generally broad with regular features, the skin a more pronounced but soft yellow, and generally better-looking ; the women especially compare very favourably in this respect with their Chinese neighbours. They would appear to be an ancient race, cut off by rugged mountains and pathless jungle from free intercourse with their neighbours, and so there has been less admixture ; a purer race (of Malay-Mongolian type) has resulted and they are generally free from the "mongrel" appearance, noticeable especially in Southern and Western China and in Western Japan, while doubtless they are at the same time wanting in the energy that "mongrel" parentage would seem to favour, where the disparity between the parents is not too wide.

Hanoi boasts a very fine bridge (supplied by a Parisian firm) which carries the railway and foot passengers across the Red River. It is cantilever, reminding us of the great Forth Bridge, is over a mile in length and spans the river proper, here about a half mile wide, together with the sand flats, rarely covered, that line the opposite bank. The deep water channel is on the Hanoi side, along the right bank, and here is a wide bund lined with scattered offices and stores; but the main residential and business quarter stands half a mile back from the river and surrounds a small lake, originally a swamp, which has been happily reclaimed and so converted into an extremely ornamental feature of this well-planned city. Another very large lake bounds the northern suburb; the site lies low and the inhabited portion has been artificially raised as in Shanghai. Hanoi has been so often described, together with the imposing scale upon which it has been laid out, as compared with the haphazard way in which British colonial towns in the Far East are left to grow of themselves, that we need not go into more detail.

Suffice it to say that, with its broad, well-kept streets, squares, cafés, and abundance of foliage, it makes a most pleasing impression and is a worthy setting to the Government of Indo-China, which now has its seat there. Nor must the streets of Annamite shops, picturesque with wonderful paper lanterns like fishes, butterflies, or crabs, be forgotten. We drove in ricshas or, as the French call them " pousse-pousses " to the Hotel Métropole, the best hotel in the Far East, magnificently appointed, furnished and decorated in excellent taste, and with a frontage of 300 feet to the street. There is also a finely situated club near by—the " Cercle de l'Union "—and a grand opera-house was being built, at a cost, we were told, of £20,000. The botanical gardens were already laid out on a large scale, affording fine shady drives and possessing a menagerie of the chief fauna of the region, including a most intelligent elephant.

A "haras," or stud-farm, was also in full operation, at which experiments on the amelioration of the breeds of domestic animals were being carried out on an imposing scale among Australian horses and Mongolian ponies ; short-horns and native cattle ; Southdowns, French

K

sheep, and those from the Yunnan plateau, together with pigs, geese, ducks, Numidian hens and barn-door fowls. Large numbers of these animals were housed in roomy buildings suitable to the climate and a wide acreage of land was laid down in pasturage for their maintenance. The superintendent, an ex-army veterinary surgeon, informed us that the pasturage was excellent and the return of reaped fodder per acre extraordinarily high, seven or eight times that of grassland in France. Our visit to this "haras" was full of interest as showing the results obtained by scientific selections of breeds, and how much is being achieved by the French authorities for the benefit of the colonists and natives of Tonking. The animals were all in excellent condition, and it was a great pleasure to see them.

The main building of the Exhibition of 1902, a well-lighted solid structure in rénaissance style, was being utilised as a museum of the natural products, arts, and manufactures of Indo-China. Thus there is plenty for the visitor to see and investigate, and we found the three days, which were all we could allot to Hanoi, far too short to do the city justice, even without visiting its environs.

Haiphong, the port of Hanoi and the centre of outer communication by rail and water for the Tonking delta generally, is distant 100 miles from the latter city and is reached in four hours' time. The railway line, whether proceeding north or south, equally leaves Hanoi by way of the great bridge over the Red River, and runs the whole way through the paddy-fields of the delta, with the high mountains (5,000 feet) that mark the frontier between Tonking and the Chinese province of Kwangtung visible in the distance, on the left. In the foreground of those mountains, as Haiphong is approached, there stands out conspicuously the curiously rugged, low ridge of limestone pinnacles which extends into the Baie d'Along, and there forms the group of picturesque rocky islets which make this bay so famous. The town of Haiphong is built on the right bank of the Cua-cam river, a stream fed from the Than-noi mountains on the north, near the Canton border; and is connected with the Red River by cross channels.

The whole country here, on the ocean edge of
the delta, is a vast low-lying swamp, from which
the site of the city has been painfully reclaimed
and which is still intersected by wide tidal
creeks. The river at this point is about a quarter
of a mile wide and fifty to sixty feet deep, and
affords good anchorage ; at the mouth, however,
which is fifteen miles distant, a sand-bar limits
the draft of vessels trading to Haiphong to
eighteen feet, but by dredging it is intended to
increase the water to twenty-four feet. Although
Haiphong boasts only some 20,000 inhabitants,
as against the 100,000 or more attributed to
Hanoi, yet the former struck us as the busier
place—more movement in its streets and more
business at its wharves—due, of course, to its
being a sea-port. The town is well laid out,
in wide streets ; as in Hanoi every provision
has been made for future expansion ; the houses
are well-built, the principal residences having
ample gardens surrounding them. The residents of Haiphong, of whom nearly 1000 are
European, enjoy further the proximity of sea
and mountain, and so possess an endless choice
of summer resorts within the compass of an

afternoon's drive on the excellent roads that surround the city.

After spending a day in Haiphong and enjoying the comparative freshness of the air there (mid-September) we embarked on board the " Marty " steamer, Hué, for Hongkong. Our passage through Tonking gave us but a glimpse of what the French were doing in this their great new colony, but with what we did see we were fairly astonished. When one considers that the French have had quiet possession of the country for barely fifteen years, the solid work that has been accomplished is truly surprising ; no labour has been spared in opening up the country to colonisation by roads and railways and in rendering the cities healthy and attractive for residence. If, as is sometimes reproached, French colonies are overdone with " function-aires," at least these are not idle ; the main criticism of one coming from British colonies is, that too little is left to individual initiative and too great demands made upon " l'administra-tion." Yet we learn from the admirable summary of Progress in Indo-China by " Pierre Padaran " that at the end of 1900 there were already 650

L

European planters engaged in tropical plantations over an area of 815,000 acres, which is equal to the sum total of European plantations in the island of Ceylon, whilst in Upper Burma, acquired by us about the same period, so far there are none.* The unoccupied mountain area open to colonisation in Indo-China is, however, infinitely greater than in either of the preceding countries ; the total area of the colony being 817,000 square kilometres (314,000 square miles), of which practically the river deltas alone are populated. The terms offered to would-be colonists are extraordinarily favourable ; while the French Administrators are now paying more attention to the outside world around them and are studying the methods of Java and Ceylon and profiting thereby. The " aléas " or drawbacks to the progress of the colony lie in the narrow spirit of the mother country—the Métropole—who would make of it a French preserve—by means of differential tariffs and by regulations

* Les possibilités Economiques de l'Indo-Chine. Paris, au siège du comité de l'Asie française, 19 Rue Bonaparte. pp. 124. —A most informing book in small compass, and though it only carries us up to 1902, it is certainly the best short account of the topography and resources of the colony of Indo-China yet published.

tending to exclude all non-French elements, be they European or Asiatic, British or Chinese— from taking part in its development. Excessive transit dues are imposed on goods from Hongkong and Singapore destined for the hinterland of Yunnan, with the impracticable design of compelling such Hinterlander to draw their supplies from direct French sources. The monopoly of supply accorded to the mother country in the colony itself enhances to residents the cost of most necessities and of all the luxuries of life, and so makes living dearer than in the neighbouring free colonies. On the other hand, it must be acknowledged that the "Métropole" spends money upon her colonial children with a lavish hand, and so is entitled to a special return ; yet, while the population of France remains stationary, this exclusive policy must greatly retard the industrial development of Indo-China, a country which, forming as it does a link between the dense population of British India on the west and the teeming millions of China on the east, and with natural resources equal to either, should, in the nature of things, develop into one of the most productive countries, if not into the greatest *entrepôt* that the world has yet seen.

We cannot take our leave of Tonking without commending it to our fellow-residents in the Far East, nor without bearing grateful testimony to the courtesy we enjoyed at all hands during our brief visit. When the Yunnan railway is in running order, Tonking will become as well-known as Japan, and then the climate of Yunnan will be found more bracing and, in summer especially, the air far drier and fresher than in Japan at that season. The total distance from Haiphong to Yunnan-fu by the new line of rail is 853 kilometers, or 533 miles ; so that, when it is completed, Hongkong will be brought within less than a week of the Yunnan sanatorium and the delightful region of its great lakes.

The steamer Hué, on which we were now bound to Hongkong, *via* Pakhoi, Hoihow, and Kwang-chouw-wan, turned out to be an old acquaintance, being one of the fine boats built by Chinese order, some sixteen years earlier, to run between Formosa and the mainland. But how fallen from her high estate ! She came out from the builders, Hawthorn, Leslie & Co. of Newcastle, as the Smith, while the Chinese christened her the Mei-shih, at which time her speed was fourteen knots and all her appointments first-class ; she now steamed ten knots only and her passenger quarters were cruelly dilapidated and ill-kept. On the third day out from Haiphong we put into the new French port, situated on the mainland of the province of Canton, Kwang-chow-wan (=Canton Bay), and were much interested in visiting this new " free port " on Chinese territory and, according to our French friends, the predestined rival to Hongkong.

The bay of Kwang-chow forms one of the finest harbours in the world, whether for trade or defence. It is entirely landlocked, an island off the mouth admitting access through two narrow entrances : once inside, it furnishes an anchorage ground ten miles by three with a depth of water of ten fathoms. After traversing this wide expanse, the bay narrows at its northern end to an arm of the sea one to two miles in width, at the head of which is the embouchure of the Kam-ho or Gold River, which descends from the range enclosing the valley of the West River on the south and marks the limit of the territory ceded

to the French in 1898. The land area of this
territory covers some 317 square miles, and
though the soil is sandy—much as at Pak-hoi,
situated on the opposite side of the Lei-chou
peninsula, eighty miles to the west—the land
is well cultivated and contains a population of
200,000 Chinese distributed in 800 villages. This
new free port is under the administration of the
Government of Indo-China, who are represented
by a local resident, together with an ample
administrative staff. As is customary with the
French, in laying out their new acquisition
grand views have prevailed and the future great-
ness of the port has been amply foreseen ; thus
one inlet had been relegated to a naval port,
and there the warships lay at anchor, out of sight
of the administrative and commercial ports.

These latter were also distinct and were established on opposite shores of the northern arm of
the bay, across which, in bad weather, as at the
time of our visit, communication was by no means
easy. The administrative town was on the left,
(treating this " arm " as the estuary of the Kam
river) or east shore, and consisted of the " Residence," the offices of the Administration and the

dwellings of the administrative staff. It also included a market with a small surrounding street of native shopkeepers. A jetty had been built, and the adjoining, mostly flat, country laid out in wide, metalled, rectangular, houseless roads, then mostly grassgrown. This Settlement, known as Matché, had a most desolate, uninhabited appearance, and, as it was there that we first landed, we received a decidedly unfavourable impression of the place ; but it is only fair to state that it had been devastated by a typhoon in the early summer. On the opposite shore was the commercial settlement and military station known as Fort Bayard, off which the " Hué " was anchored. We crossed the strait in a gale of wind and rain in one of the cockle-shell looking, but solidly built and excellent sea-boats of the place. These sail well with a single Chinese lug and, being provided with a centre-board (which is inserted before the mast and close to the bow), sail remarkably close to the wind. The " invention " of the centre-board is usually credited to a naval lieutenant 100 years back only, but it appears to have been in use in China for over 1000 years. At Hoihow, the " port "

of Kiungchow in the island of Hainan, are to be
found the best centre-board boats on the coast.
Ships there lie in the open roadstead, off a flat
sand-beach, and communicate with the shore by
means of these boats, which, being flat-bottomed,
are hauled up on the beach when not in use.

We found " Fort Bayard " a more lively place
than was the " administrative capital; " but its
liveliness was limited and only noticeable in comparison with the peaceful calm that reigned in
Matché. We put ashore at this latter place a
smart young Frenchman, a pillar of the Administration at Matché, a fellow-traveller who had
been for a visit to Haiphong. We could hardly
help envying him the retreat provided for him
—a fine climate and excellent sea bathing,—
as we left him regretfully, " the world forgetting,
by the world forgot."

Fort Bayard is built on ground that slopes to
the sea, and, the houses being less scattered than
at Matché, had more the appearance of a town,
and indeed of a well-built town. The chief
buildings were spacious barracks for the considerable garrison of French and Annamite troops
which were stationed there. The south coast of the

Canton province, exposed to the China Sea and open to the monsoons, with mountains sheltering it on the north, is exceedingly healthy ; the soil is light and porous and raised in low undulating swells well above the sea-level. Consequently the station here provides an excellent change for troops enervated by the damp heat of Tonking. We were courteously shown over the men's barracks, which were in roomy, detached buildings covering a large area of ground and affording them every comfort, not to say luxury. There was a really fine military club installed in a handsome two-storied building and open to all ranks, presented to the new colony by the all pervading M. Doumer. This late Governor of Indo-China has left his mark everywhere ; he would appear to have been a veritable " hustler ; " to him is due the equilibrium established in the budget of Indo-China, the late Hanoi exhibition, and the Yunnan railway ; he appears to have been physically and mentally untirable, we even heard of his riding from Mêng-tse to Yunnan-fu in four days ; the time by the usual stages being eleven. A new cathedral, with two towers, also adorned the Settlement, which otherwise consisted of a

street of Cantonese shops and a single French
store, well provided and selling at the moderate
prices which one expects to find in a "port
franc." The genial proprietor, M. Champestève,
we heard referred to as " *le* colon," the one serious
colonist so far of the new Hongkong.

From Kwang-chow-wan to Hongkong the
distance is 237 miles on an E.N.E. course, and
we reached our destination after a most interesting five days' coasting voyage. Our last visit
to Hongkong had been in days before the grand
foreshore reclamation scheme had been thought
of, and we were accordingly not a little astonished
at the appearance which the modern town of
Victoria now presents.

The magnificent new buildings, the crowded
piles of new offices, the throngs in the streets
and the traffic in the harbour contrasted
marvellously with the lotus-eating lands we
had been travelling through, and we felt more
than ever enamoured of free trade and of free
intercommunication for all alike. Hongkong
raises an annual revenue of six million dollars,
chiefly from land and excise taxes, and her
emergence from the barbarism of Custom-

houses is a fine object-lesson in Eastern Asia. In these days of protective tariffs and subsidised industries, we could wish that our Mother Country likewise might so arrange her revenue as to shake off the incubus of Custom-houses *in toto,* and so provide a still more striking object-lesson to her European and American neighbours than does even her marvellously successful colony on the whilom barren islet of Hongkong.

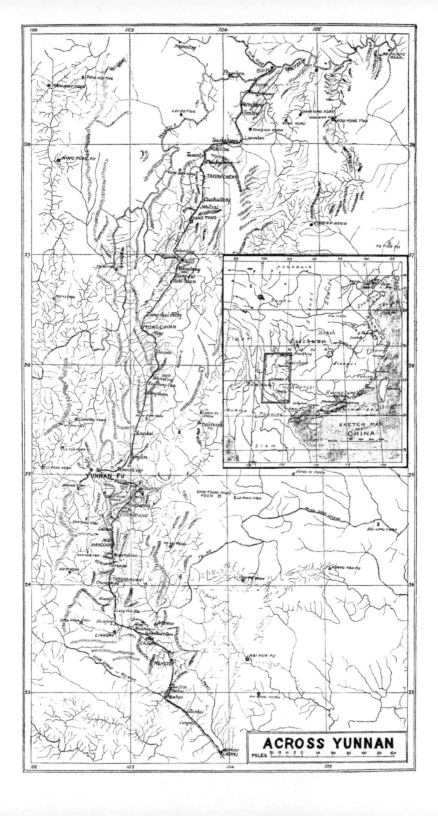

ACROSS YUNNAN

MILES

INDEX

ADOBE, Thatched, 36
Animals, Domestic, 35, 102
Annamites, Different race from
  Chinese, 125
Annamites, Good qualities of
  the, 142
Annamites, Language of the,
  135
Annamites, Make good soldiers,
  140
Anpien, Port of transhipment,
  18, 19n
Arahat Pass, 31

BAIE D'ALONG, 147
Beautiful surroundings at Chu-
  shui-tung, 31
Bible Christian Mission, 28, 36,
  46
Birds, 93, 129
Birds, Song of, 54
Bogland, 32
Boxers, Escape from, 121
Brasswork, 48
Brickfields, 29
Bridge, Cantilever, at Hanoi, 143
Bridge, Handsome suspension,
  at Kiang-ti, 38
Bridges, Fragile, 42
Bullock carts, 35

CANALS for drainage, 45
Centre-board, Ancient use of,
  155
Chao-tung city, 35
Chao-tung plain, 34
Chên-kiang, 92, 93, 94
Chên-kiang lake, 101
Chien-shan, 96
Chi-kai, town, 113
Chung-ho-pa, Basin of, 104
Chu-shui-tung, Beautiful view
  from, 31
Chu-shui-tung, Village of, 30
Clear and muddy water in one
  river, 49
Cliffs, Steps cut in, 23
Climate, Variety of, 53, 67, 70
Cloud bursts, 42, 43
Coal adits, 37
Coffins in caves, 22
Coins, Variations in value, 26
Copper articles, 47
Copper mines, 26, 46
Copper, Surreptitious trade in, 47
Cotton cloth, 26
Cultivation of the land, 70

DOCTORS, Need for, 90
Domestic animals, 35, 102
Doumer, Monsieur, 157

Drainage, Canals for, 45

EUCALYPTUS trees, 115

FELT, Red, 48
Fertility in Red River Valley, 146
Firewood from the mountains, 48
Five Stockades, Village, 32
Flowers, 15, 31, 33, 34, 37, 40, 42, 88, 93, 94, 107, 123
Food, 29
Foot binding, 45, 46
Fort Bayard, 155, 156
Free Trade, Good effects of, 158
French in Tonking, 149, 153, 154
Futai, Statue to, 80

GEOLOGICAL observations, 55
Goitre, 52, 105
Gunpowder accident, 90

HAI-MÊN-CH'IAO, 99, 100
Haiphong, Port, 147
Hanoi, 137, 141, 143
Han-yang-fu burnt down, 16
Heilungt'an, 78
Hö-k'ou, Town, 131
Hongkong, 158
Hongkong, To, Route and Distances from Yunnan-fu, vii
Hsin-chang, Village of, 21
Hsin-fang, Village, 107

IGNEOUS rocks, 56
Ijen, Aborigines, 108
Ireland, A Resemblance to, 32
Iron mines, 37

Irrigation, Artificial, At Mei-chou, 14

JUNGLE on Red River, 128

KIANG-CHUAN, 98
Kiang-ti, Village of, 38
Kuan-yi city, 105
Kwangchow, Bay of, 153

LAKES, 41
Landlordism, Baneful effects of, 46
Land, Cultivation of, 70
Land, Price of, 116
Lao-Kai, 132
Lao-wa-t'an, River, 33, 34
Lao-wa-t'an, Town of, 27
Lao-wa-t'an, Valley of the, 20
Likin stations, 26
Limestone region, 19, 23, 27, 29, 30, 33, 35, 37, 38, 39, 40, 42, 44, 49, 50, 52, 55, 60, 62, 77, 89, 96, 102, 118, 123, 147
Lin-ngan city, 108
Lohan Ling ridge, 31
Lolo, 76
Lotus ponds, 62
Lung-po, 130
Lung-shui-kou, 107
Lunpŏ, French frontier station, 124
Lu-tsung, 97

MAHOMEDAN'S, Massacre of, 72
Maize, Large fields of, 114
Malaria, 66, 120, 127
Mamelons, 123
Man-hao village, 127

Manure, Careful use of, 50
Matché, Settlement, 155
Mêng-tse, 109
Mêng-tse city, 114
Miaotse, A Hardy Race, 29
Mientien, 109
Mi-la-ti, 118
Min river, 14, 15
Mi-shin, 98
Muddy and clear water in one river, 49

NAM-TI Waterfalls, 119
Nan-hsi, 117
Nan-kwang Lake, 99, 101
Navigation, Clever, of Chinese rivers, 19
Niu-chuang, 94

OFFICIALS, Bad influence on industry, 46, 71
Opium of Yunnan, Superiority of, 104
Opium smoking, 29, 136
Opium smoking rulers, 24
Oxen used for the plough, 50

PACK animals, Trade by, 122
Paddy, 29
Peat as fuel, 32
Peat marshes, 36
Potatoes, 32
Produce, 29, 35, 38, 40, 54, 64, 102
Produce in Meic-hou district, 15
Protection, Bad effects of, 151
Railway, English, 69
Railway, French, 65, 69, 80, 82, 84, 85, 91, 108, 109, 114, 115, 117, 119, 152

Rapids, Navigation of, 128
Red earth, 36
Red River jungle, 128
Red River scenery, 129
Red River valley, Air of, 126, 128, 132, 136
Red River valley, Fertility in, 146
Ricshas, 145
Rivière Claire, 139
Rivière Noire, 139
Roads, Reasons for neglect of, 59
Roads, State of, 23, 25, 59
Rock cut gallery, 75
Rock shapes, Peculiar, 98

SAMPANS, 64
Sandstone, New Red, 56
Sandstone, Red, 27
Seed, Sowing, 50
Shale, Purple, 29, 49
Shales, 55, 94, 98
Shao-pai, Village of, 49
Shin-kai Village, 130
Shui-tien Village, 124
Siao-lung-t'an, Mountain village, 52
Silk, A common wearing apparel, 46
Silk hat covers, 26
Sowing seed, 50
Spelter mines, 26
Stalactites, Remarkable, 112
Stenches at Chinese inns, 24
Studfarm or " haras," 145
Sui-fu, Distributing mart, 16
Swallows' Cave, The, 110

TA-KUAN-CHÊNG, 22

164 INDEX

Ta-kuan River, Source of, 30
Tao-tao, Village of, 125
Ta-pan-ch'iao, 60
Ta-shui-ching, Pass of, 37
Taxes on goods, 116
Thunderstorm, Severe, 90
Tibetan plateau ascents, 26
Tieh-ling, 77
Tien-sze-pa, A filthy village, 102
Tin mines, 26, 108, 113, 115
Tonking, 149
Tonking to Hongkong, 132
Trade, Miserable conditions of, 24
Travelling, Method of, 17
Trees seen on the way, 27, 34, 37, 38, 41, 42, 51, 52, 54, 62, 78, 94, 122, 137, 141.
Tsên Yü-ying, His frequent beheadings, 73
Tsên Yü-ying Worshipped, 73
Tsung-kai, 39
Tung-chuan, 46
Tung-chuan-fu, 43
Tung-hai city, 103
Tung-hai lake, 102

VALLEYS, Fertility of the, 42
Vices undermining stamina, 73
Victoria, Hongkong, 158

Viétry, Town of, 139, 140
Villagers, Poor, and opium smokers, 29
Villages, Filthy and ruinous, 29

WAX insects, 25, 34, 37
Women planting rice, 45
Wu-tsai, Village of, 32

YA-KOU-TANG, 39
Yang-kai, 57
Yang-lin, 59
Yang-tsung-hai, Beautiful scenery round, 88
Yeh-chu-t'ang, 51
Yen-bay, 138
Yen-tse-tung, 110
Y-liang, 91
Yunnan, Climate of, 67, 70, 80
Yunnan, Description of, vii, 13, 21
Yunnan-Fu, 62
Yunnan-Fu, Excursions from, 74
Yunnan-Fu to Lao-Kai, 83
Yunnan-Fu From, to Hongkong, Route and distances, vii
Yunnan, Journey to, 14
Yunnan, Mines in, 26
Yunnan plateau, 31

For EU product safety concerns, contact us at Calle de José Abascal, 56–1°, 28003 Madrid, Spain or eugpsr@cambridge.org.

* 9 7 8 1 1 0 8 0 1 4 0 9 0 *